hamlyn

QuickCook
Desserts

Recipes by Denise Smart

Every dish, three ways – you choose!
30 minutes | 20 minutes | 10 minutes

An Hachette UK Company
www.hachette.co.uk

First published in Great Britain in 2012 by Hamlyn,
a division of Octopus Publishing Group Ltd
Endeavour House, 189 Shaftesbury Avenue
London WC2H 8JY
www.octopusbooks.co.uk

ISBN 978-0-600-62358-8

A CIP catalogue record for this book is available from the British Library

Printed and bound in China

10 9 8 7 6 5 4 3 2 1

Both metric and imperial measurements are given for the recipes. Use one set of
measures only, not a mixture of both.

Standard level spoon measurements are used in all recipes
1 tablespoon = 15 ml
1 teaspoon = 5 ml

Ovens should be preheated to the specified temperature. If using a fan-assisted oven,
follow the manufacturer's instructions for adjusting the time and temperature. Grills
should also be preheated.

This book includes dishes made with nuts and nut derivatives. It is advisable for
those with known allergic reactions to nuts and nut derivatives and those who may
be potentially vulnerable to these allergies, such as pregnant and nursing mothers,
invalids, the elderly, babies and children, to avoid dishes made with nuts and nut oils.

It is also prudent to check the labels of preprepared ingredients for the possible
inclusion of nut derivatives.

The Department of Health advises that eggs should not be consumed raw. This book
contains some dishes made with raw or lightly cooked eggs. It is prudent for more
vulnerable people such as pregnant and nursing mothers, invalids, the elderly, babies
and young children to avoid uncooked or lightly cooked dishes made with eggs.

Contents

Introduction

30 20 10 – Quick, Quicker, Quickest

This book offers a new and flexible approach to meal-planning for busy cooks, letting you choose the recipe option that best fits the time you have available. Inside you will find 360 dishes that will inspire and motivate you to get cooking every day of the year. All the recipes take a maximum of 30 minutes to cook. Some take as little as 20 minutes and, amazingly, many take only 10 minutes. With a bit of preparation, you can easily try out one new recipe from this book each night and slowly you will be able to build a wide and exciting portfolio of recipes to suit your needs.

How Does it Work?

Every recipe in the QuickCook series can be cooked one of three ways – a 30-minute version, a 20-minute version or a super-quick and easy 10-minute version. At the beginning of each chapter you'll find recipes listed by time. Choose a dish based on how much time you have and turn to that page.

You'll find the main recipe in the middle of the page accompanied by a beautiful photograph, as well as two time-variation recipes below.

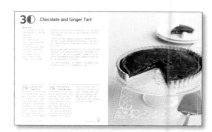

If you enjoy your chosen dish, why not go back and cook the other time-variation options at a later date? So if you liked the 20-minute Mango and Passion Fruit Tart, but only have 10 minutes to spare this time around, you'll find a way to cook it using cheat ingredients or clever shortcuts.

If you love the ingredients and flavours of the 10-minute Strawberry Eton Mess, why not try something more substantial, like the 20-minute Meringues with Strawberry Cream, or be inspired to make a more elaborate version, like the Baked Strawberry Meringue Pie? Alternatively, browse through all 360 delicious recipes, find something that catches your eye – then cook the version that fits your time frame.

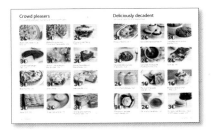

Or, for easy inspiration, turn to the gallery on pages 12–19 to get an instant overview by themes, such as Crowd Pleasers or Deliciously Decadent.

QuickCook online

To make life even easier, you can use the special code on each recipe page to email yourself a recipe card for printing, or email a text-only shopping list to your phone. Go to www.hamlynquickcook.com and enter the recipe code at the bottom of each page.

DES-HEAL-VUB

QuickCook Desserts

The busy lives that we lead today tend to leave us little time to make a delicious pudding from scratch. However, whether you fancy something fruity or chocolatey, or a dessert to tempt your family or entertain your friends, you will find something for every occasion in this book. There is also a chapter containing healthier options, so by reducing the fat and using healthier ingredients and cooking methods, you can still enjoy a delicious dessert.

The secret of the perfect dessert is to ensure you have chosen the right one as part of a meal. So if you have a heavy main course, choose a light fruity pudding, or a pastry or chocolate dessert can follow a lighter main course. The time of year will also influence your choice, so in winter you might be craving a warming comfort pudding, whereas in summer something fruitier and lighter will take your fancy. Make use of fruits when they are in season and plentiful, as they will taste so much better then, even when served simply with a scoop of ice cream or griddled with a sprinkling of sugar.

QuickCook Techniques and Tips

Anyone can make a fantastic dessert if they have the right cooking equipment to hand; a well-equipped kitchen will help you save time and get the best results.

A hand-held electric whisk is a great time-saving device when it comes to dessert-making, and makes whisking up meringues or sponges a speedy process.

A food processor is indispensable and can crush biscuits, chop nuts, blend fruit purées and coulis and make breadcrumbs, sponge mixes, biscuits and pastry in no time at all. The microwave can be used to melt chocolate and butter.

Measuring spoons and a set of scales are essential for accurate measuring. Also, make sure that you have at least two sharp knives – a small one for paring and slicing and a larger one for chopping – and remember that a sharpened knife is much safer than a blunt one. In addition, it's a good idea to invest in a selection of different-sized metal or plastic pastry cutters, an apple corer, cherry stoner, grater or microplane for removing rind from citrus fruits, pastry brushes and a rolling pin.

A selection of mixing bowls (make sure they are spotlessly clean) will be required for whisking egg whites and cream, and for mixing batters and sponge mixes.

Keep a good supply of nonstick baking sheets of different sizes, a Swiss roll tin and a supply of baking paper, foil and clingfilm. You will also need a nonstick frying pan, along with a set of saucepans.

To save time, many of these desserts are made in smaller tins, so muffin and cupcake tins, individual tart tins, ramekins, ovenproof dishes, dariole or metal pudding moulds will be required. Use the right size of tin to ensure that your desserts turn out perfectly.

QuickCook Ingredients

Make sure that your store cupboard is well stocked at all times; it's amazing how easy it is to create a quick dessert from the staple items in your kitchen larder. Cans of fruit can be made into quick crumbles or fruit fools and are a great substitute when certain fruits are out of season. Shop-bought meringue nests and shells can be quickly filled with cream and fruit, or crumbled up for a quick Strawberry Eton Mess (see page 134). Crushed biscuits make a great base for cheesecakes, can add texture to baked fruits or can be soaked in alcohol and placed in the bottom of fools or zabagliones. Cans of condensed and evaporated milk make a great substitute for fresh milk and cream and a can of caramel can be used to make a speedy Banoffee Pie (see page 130).

Always make sure that you have a supply of plain and self-raising flours, cocoa and baking powder in the cupboard. A selection of sugars, such as caster, granulated and light brown, are essential, and it's a good idea to keep some honey to hand, along with golden and maple syrups. Eggs are another staple ingredient; unless stated otherwise, all eggs used in the ingredients in this book are medium-sized.

Chocolate also appears frequently in the recipes in this book – particularly in the Heavenly Chocolate chapter. When buying dark chocolate, choose something with over 70 per cent cocoa solids, as this will help desserts to set even quicker.

Shop-bought cakes make a simple base for trifles as well as the traditional trifle sponges; alternately, make simple sponge puddings, from sliced banana, chocolate and ginger cake, baked for a short time with your favourite sauces.

Ready-made chocolate or toffee sauces, fruit compotes and coulis make great toppings for ice cream and sundaes, fillings for pancakes or bases for fruit brûlées. Ground spices such as ginger, nutmeg and cinnamon can add a delicious twist too.

Experiment with different breads, such as fruit bread, panettone and brioche, for quick bread and butter puddings, cinnamon toast or for the base of a tart.

Finally, shop-bought large or small sweet pastry cases can be quickly filled and transformed into luscious lemon, treacle or fruit tarts.

The Fridge and Freezer

Make good use of your freezer. Frozen bags of tropical fruits or summer berries can be made into crumbles, ice cream or sorbets. A short time in the freezer will help set jellies and mousses within their alloted time limit.

Today there is no need to waste precious time making your own pastry; shortcrust, puff and filo pastries can be bought chilled and frozen and transformed into fantastic desserts, such as apple or apricot tarts, millefeuilles and strudels.

Always keep in the freezer a good-quality vanilla ice cream and a fruit sorbet, so you can whip up a dessert in no time.

When making toppings for crumbles, make double and freeze one portion; that way you will always have the bare bones of a pudding to hand. When fruits are in season, stew them, then store in the freezer. These can be used for crumbles or fools.

Keep your fridge topped up, with a fresh supply of butter, milk, plain yogurt, a pot of cream or crème fraîche, cream cheese or mascarpone cheese and a chilled pot of custard, so that you will always be able to create a tasty treat. Many of these ingredients can also be used as accompaniments to serve with puddings.

Flavourings

Flavours can be easily imparted into your puddings. Buy fruit cordials, such as blackcurrant or elderflower, to add flavouring to cream or fruit syrups. For something a little more luxurious, a splash of rum or brandy, or a liqueur such as orange, blackcurrant or almond, can be added to your dessert to enhance the flavour. You can also buy cinnamon, lavender or vanilla sugars – or why not make your own vanilla sugar by placing caster sugar in a jar along with a split vanilla pod from which you have used the seeds to make a pudding?

Add a citrus kick to your dessert by whisking the grated rinds of lemons, limes and oranges in butter and sugar. Use chocolate that has been infused with ginger, orange, mint or chilli flavourings to make a speedy chocolate sauce. Buy vanilla, almond and lemon extracts rather than essences, as they have far superior flavours. More unusual flavours can be obtained from ingredients such as lemon grass, root ginger, green tea, and spices such as cardamom, cinnamon and star anise. Fresh herbs such as rosemary, basil and lemon thyme can also be used to impart aromatic flavours.

Presentation

They say the first bite is with the eye, so the way you present your desserts is of the highest importance. It takes just a few creative finishing touches to make your pudding look really luscious and professional. These can be incredibly simple, such as a dusting of icing sugar or cocoa powder, a scattering of fresh fruit or grated chocolate, or a drizzle of melted chocolate or fruit coulis. Ready-bought biscuits, such as Florentines, almond thins, macaroons, biscotti and amaretti are the perfect accompaniment to a dessert. If you have a little more time, scoop ice cream into tuile baskets (see page 236) or serve it with Salted Caramel Shards (see page 192). Or create impressive chocolate curls by spreading melted plain, white or milk chocolate about 5 mm (¼ inch) thick on a marble slab, leaving it to just set, then drawing a wallpaper scraper or knife held at a 45-degree angle across the chocolate.

Especially for summer

Delicious desserts that capture the flavours of summer.

Thai Fruit Skewers 30

Apricot and Marzipan Pastries 42

Baked Peaches with Raspberries and Amaretti 64

White Chocolate, Lemon Grass and Cardamom Mousse 104

Raspberry Millefeuille 200

Meringues with Rosewater and Pomegranate 218

Carpaccio of Pineapple with Basil 242

Griddled Mango with Lime and Chilli Syrup 252

Mango, Cardamom and Mint Fools 256

Watermelon with Mint Sugar 268

Tropical Fruit Salad with Ginger Green Tea Syrup 276

Gooseberry and Elderflower Fools 278

Winter comfort

Tasty desserts to warm you up on a cold winter day.

Spiced Oven-roasted Plums 34

Apricot and Blueberry Cobbler 50

Plum Flapjack Crumble 52

Rhubarb and Ginger Tarte Tatins 68

Chocolate Risotto 96

Bananas and Pecans with Butterscotch Custard 138

Sticky Date, Maple Syrup and Pecan Puddings 148

Mincemeat and Apple Strudel 170

Quick Rosewater and Cardamom Rice Pudding 174

Banana and Sticky Toffee Tarte Tatin 202

Spiced Dried Fruit Compote 248

Blackberry and Apple Puffs 258

Berry nice

Liven up your puddings with all things berry.

Raspberry and Honey Cranachan 26

Blueberry and Vanilla Trifles 48

Passion Fruit and Strawberry Filo Tartlets 62

Blackberry Charlotte 70

Blueberry Baskets with White Chocolate Sauce 88

Blueberry Pancakes 132

Strawberry Eton Mess 134

Sticky Blueberry and Lemon Sponge Puddings 160

White Chocolate and Raspberry Meringue Roulade 190

Easy Blackberry Fool 238

Floating Islands with Elderflower Cordial and Berries 266

Baked Red Fruit and Hazelnut Meringues 270

Chilled out

Frozen and chilled desserts, and things to pop on top.

Tropical Fruit and Basil Ice Cream 24

Chocolate Fudge Sauce 78

Chocolate and Cherry Ice Cream Sundaes 80

Chocolate Sorbet Bites 106

Rocky Road Ice Cream Sundaes 144

Chocolate and Apricot Crunch 166

Affogato al Caffe 184

Salted Caramel Shards 192

Mini Baked Alaskas 212

Coconut and Lime Jellies 214

Frozen Berry Yogurt Ice Cream 236

Instant Raspberry Sorbet 274

Kids' favourites

Make these desserts to give your kids a treat.

Sticky Poached Rhubarb on Fruit Bread 44

Sticky Pineapple Upside-down Puddings 60

Free-form Nectarine and Almond Pie 66

Pear and Chocolate Crumbles 98

Chocolate Pancakes 102

Spiced Chocolate Sponge with Belgian Chocolate Sauce 112

Fruity Chocolate Bread and Butter Pudding 120

Warm Marshmallow Dip with Fruit Skewers 142

Sesame Banana Fritters with Peanut Butter Sauce 146

Creamy Lemon and Almond Rice Pudding 154

Vanilla Poached Pears with Warm Fudge Sauce 198

Banana and Buttermilk Pancakes 260

Mini mouthfuls

Individual servings of some of your favourite desserts.

Filo Apple Pies 54

Individual Blackcurrant Cheesecakes 72

Chocolate-dipped Fruit 82

Sour Cherry Chocolate Brownie Puddings 90

Chocolate Blinis 92

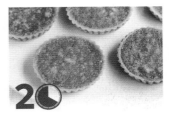

Mini Treacle Tarts 158

Baked New York Cheesecakes 164

Brandy Snaps with Limoncello Cream 204

Portuguese Custard Tarts 210

Lavender Crème Brûlées 222

Hot Mango and Passion Fruit Soufflés 224

Mini Baked Cappuccino Cheesecakes 226

Crowd pleasers

Tarts, puddings and pies to please your family and friends.

Mango and Passion Fruit Tart 38

White Chocolate and Strawberry Cheesecake 108

Chocolate and Cherry Trifle 110

Chocolate and Ginger Tart 114

Apricot, Chocolate and Brioche Tart 118

Gooey Chocolate and Prune Torte 122

Banoffee Pie 130

Sherry Trifle 150

Key Lime Pie 152

Apple Tart 162

Tangy Lemon Tarts 188

Orange and Rosemary Polenta Cake 216

Deliciously decadent

Luscious desserts for that special treat.

Cherry Clafoutis 46

Chocolate Espresso Pots 86

Chocolate and Pistachio Soufflés 116

Chocolate Mousse with Honeycomb 124

Chocolate Fondue with Hazelnut Straws 176

Tiramisu 182

Irish Coffee Syllabubs 194

Pan-fried Figs with Marsala 196

Banana and Irish Cream Trifles 206

Chocolate Cups with Mint Syllabub 208

Chocolate Zabaglione 228

Parmesan and Rosemary Thins with Poached Grapes 230

QuickCook
Fruity
Treats

Recipes listed by cooking time

30

20

 Tropical Fruit and Basil Ice Cream

Serves 4–6

450 g (14½ oz) frozen tropical
fruits, such as mango, papaya
and pineapple

1 tablespoon lime juice

200 g (7 oz) mascarpone cheese

2 tablespoons icing sugar

2 tablespoons chopped basil, plus
4–6 basil sprigs, to decorate

- Place half the fruit and the lime juice in a food processor and whizz until roughly chopped. Add the mascarpone and icing sugar and blend until fairly smooth.

- Add the remaining fruit and the basil and pulse until no large lumps of fruit remain. Scoop into bowls and serve immediately, decorated with basil sprigs.

 Tropical Ice Cream Coconut Sandwiches Make the ice cream as above and add 1 large spoonful on to one side of 1 coconut chocolate macaroon or cookie and top with another biscuit. Place in the freezer. Repeat with 10 more biscuits. Remove the ice cream sandwiches from the freezer and serve, 2 per person, immediately.

 Individual Tropical Ice Cream Bombes Make the ice cream as above and spoon into 6 x 150 ml (¼ pint) metal pudding moulds or ramekins, cover with clingfilm and freeze for 20 minutes. To serve, dip the bases of the dishes briefly in hot water and invert on to serving plates. Serve drizzled with shop-bought mango coulis.

 # Raspberry and Honey Cranachan

Serves 4

50 g (2 oz) medium oatmeal
2 tablespoons whisky
250 ml (8 fl oz) double cream
250 g (8 oz) raspberries
3 tablespoons clear honey

- Place the oatmeal in a nonstick frying pan over a medium heat and dry-fry for 2–3 minutes, stirring continuously, until toasted. Transfer to a plate to cool.

- Meanwhile, whip the whisky and cream with a hand-held electric whisk in a bowl until it forms soft peaks. Place a handful of the raspberries in a separate bowl and crush with a fork.

- Stir the oatmeal, honey, crushed raspberries and remaining raspberries into the whisky-cream. Spoon into 4 glasses and serve immediately.

 ### Oat, Raspberry and Honey Sundaes

Mix together 2 tablespoons whisky, 1 tablespoon clear honey and the grated rind and juice of ½ lemon in a small bowl. Place 300 ml (½ pint) double cream in a large bowl and pour in the honey mixture, then beat with a hand-held electric whisk until the cream starts to thicken. Divide 50 g (2 oz) honey granola between 4 glasses, then spoon 75 g (3 oz) raspberries over the granola. Spoon half the cream into the glasses. Repeat the layers, finishing with the cream. Chill for 5–10 minutes before serving.

 ### Oat and Raspberry Cranachan Trifle

Slice 2 trifle sponges in half and arrange in the base of a 15 cm (6 inch) bowl. Pour over 25 ml (1 fl oz) whisky, then scatter over 200 g (7 oz) raspberries. Top with 125 g (4 oz) granola and drizzle with 2 tablespoons clear honey. Mix together 350 g (11½ oz) shop-bought fresh vanilla custard and 1 tablespoon whisky, to taste, and pour over the granola. Lightly whip 250 ml (8 fl oz) double cream in a bowl with a hand-held electric whisk until it forms soft peaks, then spoon on top of the trifle. Decorate with extra raspberries, cover and chill for 15 minutes before serving.

Fast Fruit Brûlée

Serves 4

350 g (11½ oz) shop-bought fruit compote, such as summer fruit
500 g (1 lb) Greek yogurt
75 g (3 oz) demerara sugar

- Spoon the fruit compote into 4 x 150 ml (¼ pint) ramekins. Spoon the yogurt over the compote, then sprinkle over the sugar. Place on a baking sheet.

- Cook under a preheated hot grill for 4–5 minutes or until the sugar is brown and bubbling. Leave to cool for 3–4 minutes before serving.

 ### Tipsy Caramelized Summer Fruits

Place 450 g (14½ oz) frozen mixed summer berries in a shallow ovenproof dish. Pour over 2 tablespoons crème de cassis, then sprinkle over 2–3 tablespoons demerara sugar. Cook under a preheated hot grill for 10–15 minutes or until the sugar has caramelized. Serve with vanilla ice cream or over the Vanilla Cream Custard Pots.

Vanilla Cream Custard Pots with Fruit Compote

Chill 4 x 150 ml (¼ pint) ramekins while you make the filling. Place 3 egg yolks, 1 tablespoon custard powder, 3 tablespoons vanilla sugar and 3 tablespoons milk taken from 300 ml (½ pint) in a heatproof bowl and beat together. Warm the remaining milk in a saucepan, then gradually whisk into the egg mixture. Return to the pan and cook over a medium heat, whisking continuously, for 3–4 minutes, until the custard has thickened. Leave to cool slightly, then whisk in 150 g (5 oz) mascarpone cheese until smooth, and finally beat in a further 150 g (5 oz) mascarpone. Pour the mixture into the ramekins and chill for 15 minutes. Serve topped with 350 g (11½ oz) shop-bought fruit compote.

1⓪ Thai Fruit Skewers

Serves 4

4 long lemon grass stalks
2 kiwifruit, peeled, each cut into
   8 pieces
2 mangoes, peeled, stoned and
   cut into 1.5 cm (¾ inch) pieces
1 papaya, peeled, seeds
   removed and cut into 1.5 cm
   (¾ inch) pieces
½ pineapple, skinned, cored and
   cut into 1.5 cm (¾ inch) pieces
   (see page 242)
2 tablespoons soft light
   brown sugar
2 tablespoons desiccated coconut
vanilla yogurt, to serve (optional)

- Cut the lemon grass stalks into 20 cm (8 inch) lengths and cut each in half lengthways. Remove the tough outer layers and trim one end of each stalk to make a point (this makes skewering the fruit easier).

- Thread the fruit alternately on to 8 lemon grass skewers, then place in a single layer on a baking sheet. Mix together the sugar and coconut in a small bowl, then sprinkle over the fruit.

- Cook under a preheated hot grill for 1–2 minutes or until the sugar caramelizes and the coconut is toasted. Serve immediately, accompanied by vanilla yogurt, if using.

 Thai Fruit Skewers with Coconut Custard Prepare the fruit skewers as above. Place 200 ml (7 fl oz) coconut milk, 200 ml (7 fl oz) milk, 2 egg yolks, 2 tablespoons caster sugar and 1 teaspoon cornflour in a small saucepan. Whisk, without boiling, over a low heat for 5–10 minutes until the custard has thickened. Grill the fruit skewers as above and serve with the warm custard.

 Thai Fruit Salad in Lemon Grass Syrup Remove the tough outer layers of 2 lemon grass stalks and bash with a rolling pin to break the stalks open and release the flavour. Place in a saucepan with 150 g (5 oz) caster sugar and 200 ml (7 fl oz) water and stir over a low heat until the sugar has dissolved. When it starts to boil, take the pan off the heat and pour into a heatproof jug. Chill for 20 minutes, allowing the lemon grass to infuse, until the syrup is cold. Meanwhile, prepare the fruit as above and gently mix together in a large bowl. Strain over the syrup and stir in the juice of 2 limes. Serve immediately.

Melon and Blueberry Salad with Thyme Syrup

Serves 6

100 g (3½ oz) caster sugar
200 ml (7 fl oz) cold water
3 lemon thyme sprigs, plus extra
  to decorate
2 strips of lemon peel
½ honeydew melon
½ cantaloupe melon
½ small watermelon
150 g (5 oz) blueberries

- Place the sugar, measurement water, lemon thyme and lemon peel in a saucepan over a medium heat. Bring to the boil, then reduce the heat and simmer for 5 minutes until reduced by half.

- Leave to cool for 5 minutes, then pour into a jug and chill for a further 10 minutes. Strain the syrup to remove the lemon peel and thyme.

- Meanwhile, remove the skin and seeds from the melons and cut the flesh into cubes. Place in a bowl with the blueberries, then pour over the cooled syrup and stir well.

- Spoon into bowls with some of the syrup and serve decorated with a few sprigs of lemon thyme.

 Melon and Mint Salad

Prepare the melons as above and place in a bowl. Stir in 2 tablespoons chopped mint and the grated rind and juice of 1 lime. Sprinkle with a little sea salt and serve immediately.

 Melon, Ginger and Coriander Salad

Place 100 g (3½ oz) caster sugar, a 2.5 cm (1 inch) piece of peeled fresh root ginger, cut into thin strips, and 200 ml (7 fl oz) water in a saucepan and bring to the boil, stirring until the sugar has dissolved. Reduce the heat and simmer for 5 minutes. Pour into a heatproof jug and chill for 20 minutes. Meanwhile, remove the skin and seeds from ½ cantaloupe melon, ½ galia melon and ½ honeydew melon and cut into thin slices. Place in a bowl and strain over the cooled syrup, then scatter with 3 tablespoons chopped fresh coriander.

 Spiced Oven-roasted Plums

Serves 4

8 ripe red plums
1 cinnamon stick
2 star anise
50 g (2 oz) demerara sugar
grated rind and juice of 1 orange
2 tablespoons orange liqueur
2 tablespoons water

- Place the whole plums, cinnamon stick and star anise in a shallow ovenproof dish. Scatter over the sugar, then add the orange rind and juice, orange liqueur and measurement water.

- Place in a preheated oven, 200°C (400°F), Gas Mark 6, for 25–30 minutes, basting halfway through the cooking time.

- Spoon the plums into bowls and pour over some of the syrup. Serve immediately.

 Spiced Plum Compote

Place 500 g (1 lb) halved and pitted plums in a saucepan with 200 ml (7 fl oz) orange juice, 2 tablespoons soft light brown sugar, 1 cinnamon stick and 2 star anise. Cook, uncovered, over a low heat for 10 minutes or until the plums are tender. Remove the cinnamon stick and star anise and serve with vanilla yogurt.

Vanilla Oven-roasted Plums

Place 8 halved and pitted plums in an ovenproof dish and dot with 25 g (1 oz) unsalted butter. Sprinkle over 2 tablespoons vanilla sugar. Place in a preheated oven, 200°C (400°F), Gas Mark 6, for 10–15 minutes or until softened and caramelized. Serve with vanilla yogurt.

10 Caramelized Oranges with Cinnamon Tortillas

Serves 4

4 large oranges
75 g (3 oz) unsalted butter, slightly softened
50 g (2 oz) caster sugar
2 tablespoons icing sugar
1 teaspoon ground cinnamon
4 soft flour tortillas

- Finely grate the rind of 2 of the oranges. Using a sharp knife, cut the tops and bottoms from all the oranges and remove the skin and pith. Hold the oranges over a bowl to collect the juice and cut out the segments.

- Melt 50 g (2 oz) of the butter in a frying pan, add the caster sugar and 100 ml (3½ fl oz) of the reserved orange juice and half the rind and cook over a medium heat, stirring occasionally, until the sugar has dissolved. Simmer for 4–5 minutes until thickened and syrupy. Stir in the orange segments to heat through.

- Meanwhile, mix the remaining butter and orange rind with the icing sugar and cinnamon. Arrange the tortillas on a large baking sheet, then brush one side with the butter mixture. Place in a preheated oven, 200°C (400°F), Gas Mark 6, for 2–3 minutes or until golden. Leave to cool slightly, then cut each into 4 triangles. Spoon the oranges and syrup into bowls and serve with the tortilla triangles.

---

 20 Cinnamon Crêpes with Chocolate Orange Sauce Make 8 crêpes (see right), adding 1 teaspoon cinnamon to the batter, and keep warm. Melt 75 g (3 oz) orange-flavoured plain dark chocolate, broken into small pieces, with 150 ml (¼ pint) double cream in a heatproof bowl set over a saucepan of gently simmering water. Cut the tops and bottoms from 3 large oranges, then remove the skin and pith and cut into segments. Fold the crêpes into quarters and fill with the orange segments. Serve drizzled with the chocolate sauce.

 30 Orangey Crêpes Suzette Sift 100 g (3½ oz) plain flour and a pinch of salt into a large bowl and make a well in the centre. Pour in 2 beaten eggs, then gradually whisk into the flour. Gradually add 300 ml (½ pint) milk, whisking to form a smooth batter. Stir in 2 tablespoons melted unsalted butter. Heat a little more butter in a 20 cm (8 inch) nonstick crêpe or frying pan. Add a ladleful of batter to coat the bottom of the pan. Cook for 1–2 minutes until golden, then flip and cook for 1 minute. Repeat with the remaining batter to make 8 pancakes and keep warm. To make the syrup, place 100 g (3½ oz) softened unsalted butter and 100 g (3½ oz) caster sugar in a bowl and beat with a hand-held electric whisk until creamy, then beat in the grated rind and juice of 1 orange and 2 tablespoons orange liqueur. Place the mixture in a large frying pan and boil rapidly for 2 minutes. Reduce the heat and add the crêpes one at a time, folding each one in half and then into quarters in the syrup, until hot. Warm 2 tablespoons orange liqueur and 1 tablespoon brandy in a small pan, set alight and pour over the crêpes.

2 Mango and Passion Fruit Tart

Serves 6–8

250 g (8 oz) mascarpone cheese

25 g (1 oz) icing sugar, sifted

2 tablespoons lime juice

100 ml (3½ fl oz) canned
mango purée

20 cm (8 inch) shop-bought
sweet pastry case

1 ripe mango, peeled, stoned
and sliced

2 passion fruit

- Place the mascarpone in a bowl and beat with a wooden spoon until softened. Stir in the icing sugar, lime juice and mango purée until well combined. Spoon into the pastry case and spread the top level. Chill for 15 minutes.

- Arrange the sliced mango over the top of the tart, cut the passion fruit in half and, holding over the tart, scoop out the seeds and juice and drizzle over the mango. Serve immediately.

 **Mango and Passion
Fruit Yogurt Crunch**

Mix together 500 g (1 lb) Greek yogurt, 50 g (2 oz) sifted icing sugar and 1 tablespoon lime juice in a bowl. Peel, stone and chop 2 mangoes into small cubes and divide between 6 x 200 ml (7 fl oz) glasses. Spoon half the yogurt mixture over the top and spoon over the seeds and juice from 2 passion fruit. Scatter 75 g (3 oz) granola between the glasses and finish with the remaining yogurt and the seeds and juice from 1 passion fruit.

 **Mango and Passion
Fruit Tarte Tatin**

Place 50 g (2 oz) caster sugar, 25 g (1 oz) unsalted butter and the pulp of 2 passion fruit in a 23 cm (9 inch) frying pan with an ovenproof handle and cook over a low heat, stirring, until the butter has melted and the sugar has dissolved. Simmer for 2–3 minutes until the mixture is syrupy. Arrange 2 peeled, stoned and sliced mangoes over the syrup. Unroll a 375 g (12 oz) pack chilled ready-rolled puff pastry and cut out a circle slightly larger

than the pan. Place the circle of pastry over the pan, tucking the edges loosely round the edges so that steam can escape. Place in a preheated oven, 200°C (400°F), Gas Mark 6, for 20–25 minutes or until the pastry is puffed and golden. Leave to stand in the pan for a few minutes to cool slightly. Using an oven glove, place a serving dish on top of the pan and turn upside down. Scrape any remaining sauce over the tarte tatin.

1️⃣ Coconut Creams with Mango

Serves 4

165 ml (5½ fl oz) can
  coconut cream
250 g (8 oz) fat-free
  fromage frais
50 g (2 oz) icing sugar, sifted
2 tablespoons desiccated coconut
1 ripe mango, peeled, stoned
  and chopped

- Pour the coconut cream into a bowl, then beat in the fromage frais and icing sugar. Spoon into 4 small glasses, then chill until ready to serve.

- Meanwhile, place the desiccated coconut in a small frying pan and dry-fry over a medium heat, stirring, until lightly toasted. Leave to cool.

- Spoon the mango over the top of the coconut creams. Sprinkle over the toasted coconut and serve.

2️⃣ Griddled Mango with Coconut

Using a sharp knife, remove the skin from 2 mangoes, then cut each one into thick slices either side of the stone. Place the mango in a preheated griddle pan and cook for 5 minutes on each side. Transfer to 4 serving plates and squeeze over the juice of 2 limes. Slice the flesh of ½ coconut into thin slithers, then place in the griddle pan and cook for 1 minute on each side until toasted. Serve sprinkled over the mango.

3️⃣ Coconut Rice Pudding with

Mango Place 100 g (3½ oz) rinsed short-grain pudding rice, 3 tablespoons caster sugar and 450 ml (¾ pint) boiling water in a saucepan and bring to the boil. Reduce the heat and simmer, uncovered, for 10 minutes. Pour in 400 ml (14 fl oz) coconut milk and simmer for a further 15–20 minutes, stirring occasionally, until the rice is tender. Serve with chopped mango and toasted coconut.

20 Apricot and Marzipan Pastries

Serves 6

375 g (12 oz) pack chilled
   ready-rolled puff pastry
175 g (6 oz) marzipan,
   roughly chopped
3 tablespoons double cream,
   plus extra to serve (optional)
9 apricots, halved and stoned
25 g (1 oz) flaked almonds

- Unroll the pastry and cut into 6 x 16 x 8 cm (6½ x 3½ inch) rectangles, then place on a baking sheet. Using a sharp knife, score a 1 cm (½ inch) border around the edge, but do not cut all the way through. Prick the centre of each base with a fork. Chill while you make the filling.

- Place the marzipan and cream in a food processor or blender and blend until smooth.

- Spoon a blob of the marzipan mixture on to each pastry rectangle and spread it up to the border. Arrange 3 apricot halves on top of the marzipan, cut side up, and sprinkle over the almonds.

- Place in a preheated oven, 200°C (400°F), Gas Mark 6, for 12–13 minutes or until risen and golden. Serve warm with double cream, if using.

 Grilled Apricots with Marzipan

Halve and stone 12 apricots and arrange the halves, cut side up, in a shallow ovenproof dish. Divide 150 g (5 oz) marzipan into 24 pieces and roll into small nuggets, then place in the centres of the apricots. Sprinkle with 3 tablespoons soft light brown sugar and 25 g (1 oz) flaked almonds. Cook under a preheated hot grill for 5–6 minutes until the sugar starts to caramelize.

 Apricot and Almond Tart

Unroll a 375 g (12 oz) pack chilled ready-rolled puff pastry on to a large baking sheet, then sprinkle over 50 g (2 oz) ground almonds. Arrange about 875 g (1¾ lb) halved and stoned apricots over the top, right up to the edge of the pastry. Sprinkle over 2 tablespoons soft light brown sugar. Place in a preheated oven, 200°C (400°F), Gas Mark 6, for 20–25 minutes or until risen and golden.

1 Sticky Poached Rhubarb on Fruit Bread

Serves 4

15 g (½ oz) unsalted butter

50 g (2 oz) soft light
  brown sugar

1 teaspoon peeled and grated
  fresh root ginger

grated rind and juice of ½ orange

400 g (13 oz) rhubarb,
  trimmed and cut into 12 cm
  (5 inch) lengths

4 x 2.5 cm (1 inch) thick slices
  of fruit bread or panettone

vanilla ice cream, to serve

- Place the butter, sugar, ginger and orange rind and juice in a frying pan large enough to hold the rhubarb in a single layer and cook over a low heat until the sugar has dissolved. Add the rhubarb and simmer gently for 5 minutes, then turn over and cook for a further 2–3 minutes until tender.

- Meanwhile, lightly toast the bread. Arrange 3–4 strips of rhubarb on top of each, then drizzle over the syrup. Serve immediately with scoops of vanilla ice cream.

2 Quick Rhubarb Trifles

Place 450 g (14½ oz) rhubarb, trimmed and chopped, 50 g (2 oz) caster sugar and 1 teaspoon vanilla extract in a saucepan. Cover and simmer for 5–7 minutes until tender, then leave to cool slightly. Place 4 slices of fruit bread or panettone, cut to fit, in the bottom of 4 glasses, then spoon the rhubarb and any syrup over the top. Spoon 500 g (1 lb) pot fresh vanilla custard over the rhubarb. Lightly whip 300 ml (½ pint) double cream in a bowl with a hand-held electric whisk until it forms soft peaks, then spoon on top of the trifles. Chill until ready to serve.

3 Individual Rhubarb and Custard Pies

Place 450 g (14½ oz) rhubarb, trimmed and cut into 2.5 cm (1 inch) pieces, in a bowl and stir in 75 g (3 oz) caster sugar, 1 piece of stem ginger in syrup, finely chopped, and the grated rind of 1 orange. Spoon the rhubarb mixture and the juice into 4 x 250 ml (8 fl oz) deep ovenproof dishes and spoon 200 g (7 oz) shop-bought fresh vanilla custard over the tops. Unroll a 375 g (12 oz) pack chilled ready-rolled puff pastry and cut out 4 circles slightly larger than the dishes. Place a pastry top over the pies and brush the tops with a little beaten egg. Make a hole in the middle for the steam to escape. Place on a baking sheet and bake in a preheated oven, 190°C (375°F), Gas Mark 5, for 20–25 minutes or until golden and bubbling. Leave to stand for 5 minutes before serving.

30 Cherry Clafoutis

Serves 4

butter, for greasing
32 fresh or canned cherries, pitted
4 tablespoons kirsch
3 tablespoons caster sugar
25 g (1 oz) plain flour, sifted
4 eggs, beaten
100 ml (3½ fl oz) double cream
6 tablespoons milk
½ teaspoon vanilla extract
icing sugar, for dusting (optional)

- Grease 4 x 250 ml (8 fl oz) ramekins or ovenproof dishes and place on a baking sheet. Divide the cherries evenly between the dishes and spoon 1 tablespoon of the kirsch over each.

- Place the sugar, flour and eggs in a bowl and beat together with a hand-held electric whisk until light and well blended. Whisk in the cream, milk and vanilla extract.

- Pour the batter over the top of the cherries and place the dishes in a preheated oven, 190°C (375°F), Gas Mark 5, for 20–25 minutes or until the batter has set. Serve immediately, dusted with icing sugar, if using.

 Cherry Jubilee
Drain a 425 g (14 oz) can pitted cherries in juice, reserving the juice. Mix together 1 tablespoon of the cherry juice, 1 tablespoon caster sugar and 2 teaspoons of cornflour in a small bowl. Place the remaining cherry juice with the cornflour mixture in a frying pan and whisk until thickened, then add the cherries and warm through. Pour in 3 tablespoons warmed kirsch, then flame to burn off the alcohol. Scoop 2 large scoops of vanilla ice cream into each of 4 glasses, then pour the cherries over the top. Serve immediately.

Mini Cherry and Almond Clafoutis
Grease 8 holes of a 12-hole nonstick muffin tin and put 4 pitted cherries in the bottom of each. Place 2 tablespoons caster sugar, 2 tablespoons plain flour, 2 eggs and 1 teaspoon almond extract in a bowl and beat together with a hand-held electric whisk until blended. Whisk in 6 tablespoons double cream. Spoon the batter into the muffin tin holes and sprinkle over 2 tablespoons flaked almonds. Place in a preheated oven, 200°C (400°F), Gas Mark 6, for 12–15 minutes until risen and golden. Serve 2 clafoutis per person with a spoonful of double cream.

20 Blueberry and Vanilla Trifles

Serves 6

250 g (8 oz) blueberries,
 plus extra to decorate
25 g (1 oz) caster sugar
2 tablespoons crème de cassis
 or blackcurrant cordial
1 tablespoon water
250 g (8 oz) shop-bought
 Madeira cake, cubed
500 g (1lb) pot fresh
 vanilla custard
300 ml (½ pint) double cream
25 g (1 oz) toasted flaked almonds

- Place the blueberries, sugar, cassis or cordial and measurement water in a small saucepan and cook over a low heat, stirring, until the sugar has dissolved. Cook gently for 2–3 minutes until the berries start to burst, then pour into a bowl and chill for 10 minutes.

- Divide the cake between 6 glasses and spoon over the blueberries and their juice. Spoon the custard over the tops.

- Lightly whip the cream with a hand-held electric whisk in a bowl until it forms soft peaks, then spoon over custard. Decorate with the extra blueberries and toasted almonds. Serve immediately or chill until ready to serve.

---

10 Waffles with Blueberry and Lemon Sauce

Place 250 g (8 oz) blueberries, the grated rind and juice of 1 lemon and 50 g (2 oz) caster sugar in a saucepan and cook over a low heat, stirring, until the sugar has dissolved. Cook gently for 2–3 minutes until the berries start to burst. Meanwhile, lightly toast 6 waffles and place in bowls. Add a scoop of vanilla ice cream to each, then pour over the warm sauce and serve immediately.

---

30 Balsamic Blueberry Trifle

Place 250 g (8 oz) blueberries, 2 tablespoons caster sugar, 2 teaspoons balsamic vinegar and 1 tablespoon water in a saucepan and cook gently for 3–4 minutes until the berries start to burst, then pour into a bowl and chill for 10 minutes. Roughly chop 2 blueberry muffins and arrange in the base of a trifle bowl, then spoon over the blueberries and leave to soak. Meanwhile, blend together 25 g (1 oz) golden caster sugar, 2 teaspoons custard powder, 2 teaspoons cornflour and 1 tablespoon milk in a heatproof bowl to form a paste, then beat in 1 egg yolk. Place 325 ml (11 fl oz) milk and 1 teaspoon vanilla extract in a saucepan and heat until just below boiling point. Stir into the cornflour paste, then pour into a clean pan. Cook over a medium heat, whisking continuously, until the custard has thickened. Remove from the heat and stir in 200 ml (7 fl oz) half-fat crème fraîche until smooth. Pour into a bowl, cover with clingfilm to prevent a skin forming and chill. Spoon the chilled custard over the blueberries. Lightly whip 400 ml (14 fl oz) double cream in a bowl with a hand-held electric whisk until it forms soft peaks, then spoon on top of the trifle. Serve immediately or chill until ready to serve.

Apricot and Blueberry Cobbler

Serves 4

12 ripe apricots, halved
  and stoned
150 g (5 oz) blueberries
2 tablespoons light muscovado
  sugar
175 g (6 oz) self-raising flour,
  plus extra for dusting
50 g (2 oz) unsalted butter, diced
50 g (2 oz) caster sugar
125 ml (4 fl oz) buttermilk
milk, for brushing

- Place the apricots and blueberries in a 750 ml (1¼ pint) ovenproof dish and sprinkle over the muscovado sugar.

- Place the flour in a bowl, add the butter and rub in with the fingertips until the mixture resembles fine breadcrumbs. Stir in the caster sugar, then add the buttermilk a little at a time, to form a slightly sticky, soft dough.

- Turn the dough out on to a lightly floured surface and pat out until it is 1 cm (½ inch) thick. Cut out 8 rounds using a 6 cm (2½ inch) cutter.

- Arrange over the top of the fruit and brush with a little milk. Place in a preheated oven, 180°C (350°F), Gas Mark 4, for 20 minutes or until the scones are golden and the fruit is bubbling. Serve immediately.

 Apricot and Blueberry Compote
Place 8 halved and stoned apricots, 150 g (5 oz) blueberries, 2 tablespoons light muscovado sugar and 1 tablespoon water in a saucepan and cook over a low heat for 5–7 minutes, stirring occasionally, until the blueberries start to burst and the apricots have softened. Serve with dollops of Greek yogurt and drizzled with honey.

Speedy Apricot and Blueberry Crumbles Mix together 150 g (5 oz) blueberries and 2 drained 410 g (13 oz) cans apricot halves in juice in a bowl and sprinkle over 2 tablespoons soft light brown sugar. Spoon into 4 ovenproof dishes, then top with 225 g (7½ oz) packet crumble mix. Place on a baking sheet and bake in a preheated oven, 190°C (375°F), Gas Mark 5, for 15 minutes or until golden and bubbling.

30 Plum Flapjack Crumble

Serves 6

1 kg (2 lb) ripe plums, about
    9–10 plums depending on size,
    halved and pitted
1 teaspoon vanilla extract
2 tablespoons soft light
    brown sugar
custard, to serve (optional)

For the topping

150 g (5 oz) unsalted butter
150 ml (¼ pint) golden syrup
½ teaspoon salt
200 g (7 oz) rolled oats
25 g (1 oz) flaked almonds

- To make the topping, gently melt the butter, golden syrup and salt in a saucepan. Remove from the heat and stir in the oats and almonds.

- Meanwhile, cut the plums into quarters, or smaller if large. Place in an ovenproof dish and sprinkle over the vanilla extract and sugar.

- Pile the topping over the plums, allowing some of the fruit to poke through. Place in a preheated oven, 190°C (375°F), Gas Mark 5, for 25 minutes or until the topping is golden and the plums have softened. Serve with custard, if using.

 1 Plum, Yogurt and Granola Layer

Pit and quarter 12 plums and divide between 6 glasses. Divide 300 g (10 oz) granola between the glasses and spoon 50 g (2 oz) vanilla yogurt over each. Serve immediately.

 2 Individual Red Plum Crumbles

Divide 2 x 570 g (1¼ lb) cans plums in syrup between 6 shallow ovenproof dishes, halving the plums if necessary, and spoon 4 tablespoons of the syrup over each. Make the flapjack crumble topping as above, then pile over the plums. Place on a baking sheet and bake in a preheated oven, 190°C (375°F), Gas Mark 5, for 10–12 minutes or until golden and bubbling.

30 Filo Apple Pies

Serves 6–8

650 g (1 lb 5 oz) Bramley apples, peeled, cored and cut into 1 cm (½ inch) pieces

100 g (3½ oz) light muscovado sugar

grated rind and juice of ½ lemon

½ teaspoon ground cinnamon

50 g (2 oz) sultanas

200 g (7 oz) filo pastry

50 g (2 oz) unsalted butter, melted

icing sugar, for dusting

vanilla ice cream or single cream, to serve (optional)

- Place the apples, sugar, lemon rind and juice, cinnamon and sultanas in a large saucepan and cook gently for 5 minutes, stirring occasionally, until the apples have softened but still hold their shape. Leave to cool slightly.

- Meanwhile, cut the pastry into 32 x 14 cm (5½ inch) squares, reserving the trimmings. Cover the pastry with a damp cloth to prevent it drying out. Take one of the squares and brush with butter, then place another square over the top at an angle to make a star shape. Repeat with 2 more squares of pastry, brushing each with butter. Gently press into a hole of a 12-hole nonstick muffin tin. Repeat with the remaining pastry to make 8 pastry cases.

- Fill each case with the apple mixture, then brush the trimmings with butter, scrunch up and place on top of the pies. Place in a preheated oven, 190°C (375°F), Gas Mark 5, for 15 minutes or until golden brown. Serve 1–2 pies per person, dusted with icing sugar and accompanied by scoops of vanilla ice cream or single cream, if using.

 Apple and Blackberry Compote Melt 50 g (2 oz) unsalted butter in a large saucepan. Stir in 50 g (2 oz) caster sugar, then add 550 g (1 lb 2 oz) peeled, cored and chopped dessert apples and 2 tablespoons Calvados or apple juice. Cook for 4–5 minutes, stirring, until the apples are golden brown and tender. Stir in 225 g (7½ oz) blackberries and cook for a further 3–4 minutes until they start to release their juice. Serve with vanilla ice cream.

 Baked Bramley Apple Rings Keeping the apples whole, peel and core 6 small Bramley apples, then cut each into 4 thick rings. Place in a buttered roasting tin. Mix together ½ teaspoon ground cinnamon, ½ teaspoon ground ginger, 3 tablespoons honey and 150 g (5 oz) raisins in a bowl and spoon the mixture into the centre of the apples. Add 4 tablespoons water and place in a preheated oven, 200°C (400°F), Gas Mark 6, for 15 minutes.

30 Rhubarb, Orange and Almond Crumbles

Serves 4

400 g (13 oz) rhubarb,
 trimmed and cut into 2.5 cm
 (1 inch) pieces
75 g (3 oz) caster sugar
juice of 1 small orange

For the topping

125 g (4 oz) plain flour
75 g (3 oz) unsalted butter, diced
4 tablespoons caster sugar
4 tablespoons ground almonds
grated rind of 1 small orange

- Place the rhubarb, sugar and orange juice in a large bowl and stir well.

- To make the topping, place the flour in a bowl, add the butter and rub in with the fingertips until the mixture resembles fine breadcrumbs. Alternatively, use a food processor. Stir in the sugar, almonds and orange rind.

- Spoon the rhubarb mixture and juice into 4 x 250 ml (8 fl oz) ovenproof dishes. Sprinkle over the topping and press down lightly.

- Place on a baking sheet and bake in a preheated oven, 190°C (375°F), Gas Mark 5, for 20–25 minutes or until golden and bubbling.

 Speedy Rhubarb and Orange Compote Place 400 g (13 oz) rhubarb, prepared as above, the grated rind and juice of 1 small orange and 2 tablespoons caster sugar in a saucepan. Cover with a lid and simmer for 5–7 minutes until tender. Serve warm, spooned over vanilla ice cream.

 Rhubarb and Orange Fools Place 400 g (13 oz) rhubarb, prepared as above, with 75 g (3 oz) caster sugar, the grated rind of ½ orange and 1 tablespoon orange juice in a saucepan and simmer for 8–10 minutes until tender. Leave to cool slightly, then place in a food processor or blender with 225 g (7½ oz) shop-bought fresh custard and blend until well combined. Spoon into 4 glasses and chill until ready to serve. Serve topped with a handful of toasted flaked almonds.

30 Orange and Cranberry Puddings

Serves 4

100 g (3½ oz) unsalted butter,
 softened, plus extra
 for greasing
grated rind of ½ small orange
100 g (3½ oz) caster sugar
1 tablespoon golden syrup
2 eggs
125 g (4 oz) self-raising flour,
 sifted
75 g (3 oz) dried cranberries
whipped cream, to serve

For the sauce

3 tablespoons chunky orange
 marmalade
1 tablespoon cranberry jelly
2 tablespoons orange juice

- To make the sauce, place all the ingredients in a saucepan and heat gently until the marmalade and cranberry jelly are dissolved. Bring to the boil, then reduce the heat and simmer gently for 5 minutes to form a thick syrup.

- Meanwhile, grease 4 x 200 ml (7 fl oz) ramekins or metal pudding moulds and line the base with nonstick baking paper. Place on a baking sheet and spoon the sauce into the bottom of each.

- Place the butter, orange rind, sugar and golden syrup in a large bowl and beat together with a hand-held electric whisk until light and fluffy. Beat in the eggs, one at a time, then gently fold in the flour and cranberries.

- Spoon the pudding mixture into the dishes and place in a preheated oven, 190°C (375°F), Gas Mark 5, for 20 minutes or until risen and set.

- Turn out the puddings on to serving plates and serve with dollops of whipped cream.

1 Orange and Cranberry Purée

Place 125 g (4 oz) caster sugar and 150 ml (¼ pint) fresh orange juice in a saucepan and stir over a low heat until the sugar has dissolved. Add 250 g (8 oz) cranberries and cook over a low heat for 7–8 minutes until the cranberries have popped. Place in a food processor or blender and blend to form a purée, then press through a sieve into a bowl. Delicious stirred into yogurt.

2 Individual Orange and Cranberry Upside-down Cakes

Melt 15 g (½ oz) butter in a frying pan and add 25 g (1 oz) caster sugar. Stir in 100 g (3½ oz) cranberries and cook for 2–3 minutes until syrupy. Spoon the mixture into 4 greased holes of a 6-hole nonstick muffin tin. Meanwhile, place 75 g (3 oz) self-raising flour, 75 g (3 oz) caster sugar, 75 g (3 oz) softened unsalted butter, the grated rind of 1 orange and 1 egg in a food processor or blender and blend until combined. Spoon the mixture over the berries. Place in a preheated oven, 180°C (350°F), Gas Mark 4, for 12–15 minutes until risen and golden. Turn out the cakes on to serving plates and serve warm.

30 Sticky Pineapple Upside-down Puddings

Serves 4

25 g (1 oz) unsalted butter
50 g (2 oz) soft light brown sugar
4 canned pineapple rings in juice,
   drained
4 glacé cherries

For the sponge

100 g (3½ oz) unsalted butter,
   softened, plus extra
   for greasing
100 g (3½ oz) caster sugar
2 eggs
175 g (6 oz) self-raising flour
¼ teaspoon ground mixed spice

- Lightly grease 4 x 200 ml (7 fl oz) ramekins or metal pudding moulds and place on a baking sheet.

- Melt the butter in a small saucepan, add the sugar and cook until the sugar has dissolved. Pour into the prepared dishes, then place a pineapple ring in each dish and a cherry in the centre of each ring.

- To make the sponge, place the butter and sugar in a large bowl and beat together with a hand-held electric whisk until light and fluffy, then beat in the eggs. Gently fold in the flour and mixed spice.

- Spoon the mixture into the dishes and spread the tops level. Place in a preheated oven, 180°C (350°F), Gas Mark 4, for 20 minutes or until risen and firm to the touch. Leave to cool in the tins for a few minutes.

- Turn out the puddings on to plates and serve immediately.

 Grilled Cinnamon Pineapple Rings

Cut the top and base off 1 pineapple. Hold the pineapple firmly, resting it on the cut base. Slice off the skin, working from top to bottom, removing any brown 'eyes'. Cut into 1 cm (½ inch) thick rounds and remove the tough central core using an apple corer. Mix together 3 tablespoons soft light brown sugar and 1 teaspoon ground cinnamon on a plate. Dip the pineapple rings in 50 g (2 oz) melted unsalted butter, then coat in the cinnamon sugar mixture. Place on a baking sheet and cook under a preheated hot grill for 3–4 minutes or until caramelized.

 Pineapple in Warm Spiced Syrup

Place 100 g (3½ oz) caster sugar, 2.5 cm (1 inch) piece of peeled fresh root ginger, cut into thin strips, 1 cinnamon stick and 200 ml (7 fl oz) water in a small saucepan and bring to a gentle simmer, stirring until the sugar has dissolved. Remove from the heat and stir in the juice of 1 lemon. Slice the skin from the pineapple (see left). Cut into quarters lengthways, remove the tough central core and cut into thick slices. Place in a heatproof bowl and pour over the warm syrup. Leave for 15 minutes to cool slightly.

Passion Fruit and Strawberry Filo Tartlets

Serves 6

200 g (7 oz) filo pastry
1 tablespoon sunflower oil
150 g (5 oz) mascarpone cheese
1 tablespoon icing sugar, plus
  extra for dusting (optional)
2 passion fruit
100 g (3½ oz) strawberries,
  hulled and sliced

- Cut the pastry into 24 x 12 cm (5 inch) squares. Cover the pastry with a damp cloth to prevent it drying out. Take one of the squares of pastry and brush with a little oil. Place another square over the top at an angle to make a star shape. Repeat with 2 more squares of pastry, brushing each with oil. Gently press into a hole of a 6-hole nonstick muffin tin. Repeat with the remaining pastry to make 6 pastry cases.

- Place in a preheated oven, 180°C (350°F), Gas Mark 4, for 5 minutes or until golden. Remove the cases from the tin and cool on a wire rack.

- Meanwhile, place the mascarpone and icing sugar in a bowl and beat together. Cut the passion fruit in half and scoop the juice and seeds into the mixture. Stir well, then spoon into the cooled cases.

- Decorate with the strawberries and dust with icing sugar, if using. Serve immediately.

 Warm Passion Fruit Curd Tartlets Place 125 ml (4 fl oz) passion fruit pulp (about 5 passion fruit) and 100 g (3½ oz) unsalted butter in a saucepan over a low heat and stir until the butter has melted. Whisk in 75 g (3 oz) caster sugar, 1 whole egg and 3 egg yolks, then cook over a low heat, whisking continuously, for 5–6 minutes until the mixture has thickened. Fill 6 x 8 cm (3½ inch) shop-bought sweet pastry cases with the passion fruit curd and serve warm with hulled and sliced strawberries.

 Shortcake with Passion Fruit and Mascarpone Cream Place 250 g (8 oz) self-raising flour in a bowl, add 50 g (2 oz) diced unsalted butter and rub in with the fingertips until the mixture resembles fine breadcrumbs. Stir in 50 g (2 oz) caster sugar and 125–150 ml (4–5 fl oz) milk and mix to form a soft dough. Turn out on to a lightly floured surface and knead briefly until smooth. Roll out and gently press into a greased 20 cm (8 inch) loose-bottomed round cake tin. Place in a preheated oven, 200°C (400°F), Gas Mark 6, for 15–20 minutes or until risen, firm to the touch and golden brown. Leave to cool in the tin for 5 minutes, then turn out on to a wire rack and cool completely. Meanwhile, make the mascarpone and passion fruit mixture as above and serve with the shortcake, decorated with hulled and sliced strawberries.

Baked Peaches with Raspberries and Amaretti

Serves 4

4 ripe peaches, halved and stoned
125 g (4 oz) raspberries
250 g (8 oz) mascarpone cheese
1 tablespoon almond liqueur
6 amaretti biscuits, crushed
2 tablespoons honey

- Place the peach halves in a shallow ovenproof dish, cut side up. Spoon the raspberries into the centres and over the top.

- Mix together the mascarpone, almond liqueur and crushed biscuits in a bowl, then spoon over the peaches. Drizzle with the honey.

- Place in a preheated oven, 200°C (400°F), Gas Mark 6, for 10 minutes or until the mascarpone has melted.

- Spoon the peaches into bowls, spooning over the sauce and raspberries, and serve immediately.

Simple Peach Melba

Drain 8 canned peach halves and place 2 halves in each of 4 glasses. Place 300 g (10 oz) raspberries, 50 g (2 oz) icing sugar and 2 teaspoons lemon juice in a food processor or blender and blend to form a purée, then press through a sieve into a bowl to remove the pips. Add a scoop of vanilla ice cream to each of the glasses and drizzle with the raspberry sauce. Serve immediately.

Peach and Raspberry Pudding

Halve, stone and slice 2 peaches and arrange in the bottom of a shallow ovenproof dish. Add 150 g (5 oz) raspberries and crumble over 6 amaretti biscuits. Mix together 250 g (8 oz) mascarpone cheese, 1 tablespoon almond liqueur and 2 tablespoons caster sugar in a bowl. Spoon over the fruit and sprinkle the top with 2 tablespoons demerara sugar. Place in a preheated oven, 180°C (350°F), Gas Mark 4, for 20 minutes.

30 Free-form Nectarine and Almond Pie

Serves 4–6

500 g (1 lb) pack chilled
  all-butter puff pastry
flour, for dusting
4 tablespoons ground almonds
6 ripe nectarines, halved, stoned
  and quartered
1 beaten egg
2 tablespoons demerara sugar
2 tablespoons flaked almonds
icing sugar, for dusting
double cream, to serve (optional)

• Roll out the pastry on a lightly floured surface to about a 30 cm (12 inch) round and place on to a large baking sheet. Sprinkle over the ground almonds, then pile the nectarines in the centre of the pastry.

• Brush the edges of the pastry with a little of the beaten egg, then bring the pastry edges into the centre, leaving the fruit exposed in the middle. Scrunch up the edges of the pastry, then brush with more beaten egg. Sprinkle over the sugar and flaked almonds.

• Place in a preheated oven, 200°C (400°F), Gas Mark 6, for 20–25 minutes or until the pastry is browned.

• Dust the warm pie with icing sugar and serve in slices with double cream, if using.

 1 **Hazelnut Cream Shortbreads with Nectarines** Lightly whip 150 ml (¼ pint) double cream in a bowl with a hand-held electric whisk until it forms soft peaks. Stir in 25 g (1 oz) chopped toasted hazelnuts, then spoon on top of 8–12 shortbread biscuits. Halve and stone 2 nectarines and cut into slices. Arrange over the cream and serve immediately.

2 **Baked Nectarines with Pistachios and Almonds** Halve and stone 4 ripe nectarines and place in a buttered ovenproof dish, cut side up. Place 50 g (2 oz) shelled pistachio nuts, 75 g (3 oz) macaroons and 25 g (1 oz) soft light brown sugar in a food processor and pulse to form fine breadcrumbs. Add 50 g (2 oz) softened unsalted butter and 50 g (2 oz) marzipan and whizz to form a paste. Spoon a tablespoon of the mixture into each nectarine cavity and drizzle 2 tablespoons almond liqueur over the top. Scatter with 2 tablespoons flaked almonds and place in a preheated oven, 200°C (400°F), Gas Mark 5, for 15 minutes or until softened and golden.

 # Rhubarb and Ginger Tarte Tatins

Serves 4

4 sticks of rhubarb, trimmed and
cut into 2.5 cm (1 inch) pieces
25 g (1 oz) unsalted butter
2 pieces of stem ginger in syrup,
finely chopped
4 tablespoons stem ginger syrup
(taken from the jar)
375 g (12 oz) pack chilled
ready-rolled puff pastry
vanilla ice cream or single cream,
to serve (optional)

- Divide the rhubarb between 4 x 10 cm (4 inch) tarte tatin
or metal pie dishes. Place the butter, chopped stem ginger
and stem ginger syrup in a small saucepan and bring to the
boil. Pour the ginger mixture evenly over the rhubarb.

- Unroll the pastry and cut out circles using a cutter slightly
larger than the dishes. Place the pastry circles over the
dishes, tucking the edges loosely round the edges so that
steam can escape.

- Place in a preheated oven, 200 °C (400°F), Gas Mark 6, for
10–12 minutes or until the pastry is puffed and golden. Leave
to stand in the dishes for a few minutes to cool slightly.

- Using an oven glove, place a serving plate on top of each
dish and turn upside down. Scrape any remaining sauce in
the dishes over the tarte tatins. Serve immediately with
vanilla ice cream or single cream, if using.

Rhubarb and Ginger Compote

Place 450 g (14½ oz)
rhubarb, prepared as above,
in a saucepan with 2 pieces of
stem ginger in syrup, chopped,
2 tablespoons stem ginger syrup
and 1 tablespoon caster sugar.
Cover with a lid and cook over
a low heat for 7–10 minutes,
stirring occasionally, until
tender. Serve warm with
dollops of Greek yogurt.

Individual Rhubarb and Ginger

Crumbles Place 700 g (1 lb 7 oz)
rhubarb, prepared as above,
in a bowl with 2 pieces of stem
ginger in syrup, finely chopped,
2 tablespoons stem ginger syrup
and 25 g (1 oz) caster sugar.
Mix together and spoon into
4 x 250 ml (8 fl oz) ovenproof
dishes. Place 175 g (6 oz) plain
flour and 50 g (2 oz) rolled oats
in a bowl, add 100 g (3½ oz)
diced unsalted butter and
rub in with the fingertips until
the mixture resembles fine
breadcrumbs. Alternatively,
use a food processor. Stir in
50 g (2 oz) caster sugar and
sprinkle over the rhubarb. Place
on a baking sheet and bake in a
preheated oven, 180°C (350° F),
Gas Mark 4, for 20–25 minutes
or until bubbling.

30 Blackberry Charlotte

Serves 4

500 g (1 lb) blackberries
150 g (5 oz) caster sugar
1 teaspoon vanilla extract
8 small, thin slices of white bread
25 g (1 oz) unsalted butter,
    softened
custard, to serve (optional)

- Place the blackberries in an ovenproof dish, then gently stir in the sugar and vanilla extract.

- Cut the crusts from the bread, spread both sides with the butter and cut in half to form triangles. Arrange over the blackberries, overlapping slightly in 2 rows.

- Place in a preheated oven, 190°C (375°F), Gas Mark 5, for 20–25 minutes or until the bread is golden and crisp and the fruit bubbling. Serve with custard, if using.

 **Blackberry Compote**

Place 450 g (14½ oz) blackberries, 125 g (4 oz) caster sugar and 3 tablespoons crème de cassis in a saucepan and cook over a low heat, stirring, until the sugar has dissolved. Simmer for 4–5 minutes until the blackberries have softened and started to release their juice. Serve spooned over vanilla ice cream.

 Individual Blackberry Charlotte Puddings

Place 400 g (13 oz) blackberries and 150 g (5 oz) caster sugar in a saucepan and cook for 2–3 minutes or until the blackberries have started to break down. Cut the crusts from 12 slices of white bread, then, using a cutter, stamp out 4 circles to fit the mould bases and 4 larger circles for the tops. Cut the remaining bread into strips. Dip each piece of bread in 125 g (4 oz) melted unsalted butter and use to line the bottom and sides of the moulds. Spoon the blackberries and any juice into 4 greased dariole moulds, then top with the larger circles of bread. Place on a baking sheet and bake in a preheated oven, 200°C (400°F), Gas Mark 6, for 8–10 minutes or until golden. Leave to cool in the tins for a few minutes. Turn out the puddings into bowls and serve with custard.

3 Individual Blackcurrant Cheesecakes

Serves 6

100 g (3½ oz) digestive biscuits, crushed

50 g (2 oz) unsalted butter, melted

135 g (4½ oz) pack blackcurrant jelly, cut into small pieces

100 ml (3½ fl oz) boiling water

100 ml (3½ fl oz) evaporated milk, chilled

100 g (3½ oz) soft cream cheese

75 g (3 oz) frozen blackcurrants

a few fresh blackcurrants, to decorate

- Stir the crushed biscuits into the melted butter and press into the bases of 6 x 8 cm (3½ inch) loose-bottomed round tart tins. Chill while you make the filling.

- Place the jelly in a heatproof jug and pour over the measurement water. Stir until it is fully dissolved.

- Whisk the evaporated milk in a large bowl with a hand-held electric whisk until light and fluffy and doubled in volume. Whisk in the cream cheese, until there are no lumps and the mixture is smooth, then whisk in the jelly. Stir in the blackcurrants and mix well.

- Pour over the biscuit bases and leave to chill for 15 minutes or until set. Serve decorated with extra blackcurrants.

 Blackcurrant Coulis Place 225 g (7½ oz) blackcurrants and 75 g (3 oz) caster sugar in a food processor or blender and blend until smooth, then press through a sieve into a bowl. Serve the coulis poured over ice cream.

 Blackcurrant Milk Jellies Place a 135 g (4½ oz) pack blackcurrant jelly in a heatproof jug and pour over 100 ml (3½ fl oz) boiling water. Stir until it is fully dissolved. Whisk a chilled 410 g (13 oz) can evaporated milk in a large bowl with a hand-held electric whisk until doubled in volume, then whisk in the jelly. Stir in 100 g (3½ oz) frozen blackcurrants, until they start to release their juice, then pour into 6 glasses. Chill for 10 minutes until set.

QuickCook

Heavenly
Chocolate

Recipes listed by cooking time

30

20

10

Chocolate Fudge Sauce

Serves 6

200 ml (7 fl oz) double cream
150 g (5 oz) light muscovado
 sugar
25 g (1 oz) unsalted butter
4 tablespoons golden syrup
125 ml (4 fl oz) milk
200 g (7 oz) plain chocolate
 (72% cocoa solids), broken
 into small pieces
ice cream, to serve

- Place the cream, sugar, butter, golden syrup and milk in a heavy-based saucepan and heat gently until the sugar has dissolved and the butter has melted. Bring to the boil, then boil for 5 minutes, stirring continuously, until thick and smooth.

- Remove from the heat, add the chocolate and stir until melted. Leave to cool slightly, then pour over ice cream.

 Knickerbocker Glories with Chocolate Fudge Sauce

Make the sauce as above. Chop 3 double chocolate muffins and divide half between 6 tall sundae glasses. Add 1 large scoop of strawberry ice cream to each glass and top with 3 hulled and halved strawberries. Drizzle 2 tablespoons of the warm sauce over each sundae, then repeat the layers, finishing with the sauce. Serve each sundae decorated with a strawberry.

Simple Gooey Chocolate Fudge Pudding Make the sauce as above. Meanwhile, slice a 350 g (11½ oz) shop-bought chocolate cake into 1 cm (½ inch) thick slices and arrange in the bottom of a 900 ml (1½ pint) ovenproof dish. Spoon over 250 ml (8 fl oz) of the sauce. Place in a preheated oven, 180°C (350°F), Gas Mark 4, for 20 minutes or until bubbling.

Chocolate and Cherry Ice Cream Sundaes

Serves 4

450 g (14½ oz) cherries, halved and pitted

4 tablespoons kirsch or cherry syrup

500 g (1 lb) tub vanilla ice cream

2 double chocolate muffins, roughly chopped

100 ml (3½ fl oz) shop-bought Belgian chocolate sauce

300 ml (½ pint) whipping cream

To serve

4 cherries on their stems
a little grated chocolate

- Place a few of the cherries in the bottom of 4 tall sundae glasses and spoon 1 tablespoon of the kirsch or cherry syrup into each glass. Add 2 small scoops of vanilla ice cream to each glass. Divide half the muffin pieces between the glasses and spoon 1 tablespoon chocolate sauce over each.

- Repeat with another layer of cherries, ice cream, muffins and chocolate sauce, finishing with an extra layer of cherries.

- Lightly whip the cream in a bowl with a hand-held electric whisk until soft peaks form and spoon over the sundaes. Decorate with the cherries on their stalks and a little grated chocolate. Serve immediately with long spoons.

2 **Cherry and Chocolate Brownie Squares** Cut 4 shop-bought chocolate brownies in half crossways to make thin slices. Lightly whip 300 ml (½ pint) double cream with a hand-held electric whisk in a bowl until it forms soft peaks, then spread half the whipped cream over 4 of the brownie squares. Top each one with 3 cherries taken from a jar of cherries in kirsch, then top with the remaining brownie slices. Press down lightly, then spoon the remaining cream on top and top with 3 more cherries and a drizzle of the kirsch. Chill for 10 minutes before serving to allow the flavours to mingle.

3 **Tipsy Cherry and Chocolate Puddings** Divide 400 g (13 oz) pitted cherries between 4 small tumblers. Place 4 large egg yolks, 25 g (1 oz) cocoa powder and 75 g (3 oz) caster sugar in a large heatproof bowl and beat with a hand-held electric whisk until thick and creamy. Set the bowl over a saucepan of simmering water and gradually whisk in 100 ml (3½ fl oz) Marsala. Continue whisking for a further 10 minutes or until the mixture has thickened. Remove from the heat and whisk for a few more minutes. Pour over the cherries and serve immediately.

Chocolate-dipped Fruit

Serves 6

75 g (3 oz) white chocolate, broken into small pieces

75 g (3 oz) plain dark chocolate, broken into small pieces

400 g (13 oz) strawberries, with stems

125 g (4 oz) cherries, with stems

125 g (4 oz) Cape gooseberries

- Melt the chocolate in 2 separate heatproof bowls set over saucepans of gently simmering water, then leave to cool slightly.

- Line a baking sheet with nonstick baking paper. Half-dip a selection of the fruit in the dark chocolate and allow the excess to drip back into the bowl. Place on the baking sheet to set. Half-dip the remaining fruit in the white chocolate and place on the baking sheet. Chill for 10–15 minutes until set.

White Chocolate Dipping Sauce with Fruit Place 200 g (7 oz) roughly chopped white chocolate, broken into small pieces, 150 ml (¼ pint) double cream, 50 g (2 oz) diced unsalted butter and 1 teaspoon vanilla extract in a small heatproof bowl set over a saucepan of simmering water. Heat gently for 5–7 minutes, stirring occasionally, until smooth and glossy. Pour into a warm bowl and serve immediately with 400 g (13 oz) strawberries, with stems, 125 g (4 oz) cherries, with stems, and 1 large sliced banana for dipping.

Chocolate Fruit Bowl Melt 225 g (7½ oz) plain dark chocolate, broken into small pieces, in a heatproof bowl set over a saucepan of gently simmering water. Meanwhile, lay 2 x 28 cm (11 inch) square pieces of heavy-duty foil together and fold the edges over to secure, then place over an upturned 600 ml (1 pint) pudding basin. Mould the foil around the bowl, smoothing out to remove the creases. Carefully remove the foil from the bowl and turn the right way up and flatten out the base. Using a spoon, spread the chocolate over the inside of the foil, leaving a ragged edge at the top. Place in the freezer for 10 minutes to firm up, then chill for 10 minutes until set. Just before serving, quickly and carefully remove the foil and fill with 400 g (13 oz) strawberries, with stems, 125 g (4 oz) cherries, with stems, and 125 g (4 oz) Cape gooseberries.

1 Chocolate and Mandarin Cheesecakes

Serves 4

300 g (10 oz) can mandarins in juice
1 tablespoon caster sugar
75 g (3 oz) milk chocolate, broken into small pieces
4 digestive biscuits, crushed
150 g (5 oz) cream cheese
125 ml (4 fl oz) double cream

- Drain the mandarins, reserving 100 ml (3½ fl oz) of the juice. Place the reserved juice and sugar in a small saucepan and simmer for 3–4 minutes. Leave to cool.

- Meanwhile, melt the chocolate in a heatproof bowl set over a saucepan of gently simmering water, then leave to cool. Divide the crushed biscuits between 4 x 150 ml (¼ pint) glasses.

- Place the cream cheese and double cream in a bowl and whisk together until just combined, then stir in the chocolate. Spoon into the glasses.

- Top with the mandarin slices, then drizzle over the cooled syrup. Serve immediately.

2 Mandarin and Chocolate Fools

Melt 125 g (4 oz) plain or orange-flavoured dark chocolate, broken into small pieces, in a heatproof bowl set over a saucepan of gently simmering water, then leave to cool. Place 300 ml (½ pint) shop-bought fresh custard in a bowl and stir in the melted chocolate. Drain a 300 g (10 oz) can mandarins in juice and divide between 4 glasses. Top with the chocolate custard and chill for 10 minutes. Serve decorated with chocolate curls.

3 Upside-down Mandarin and Chocolate Cake

Drain 2 x 300 g (10 oz) cans mandarins in juice. Arrange the mandarins over the base of a 20 cm (8 inch) loose-bottomed round cake tin lined with nonstick baking paper. Place 2 eggs and 75 g (3 oz) caster sugar in a large bowl and beat with a hand-held electric whisk until pale and thick and the whisk leaves a trail when lifted above the mixture. Sift in 50 g (2 oz) self-raising flour and 25 g (1 oz) cocoa powder and gently fold in. Pour over the mandarins and place in a preheated oven, 180°C (350°F), Gas Mark 4, for 20–25 minutes or until firm to the touch. Leave to cool in the tin for a few minutes, then invert on to a plate and serve in slices.

20 Chocolate Espresso Pots

Serves 4

125 g (4 oz) plain dark chocolate (75–80% cocoa solids), broken into small pieces
2 teaspoons espresso powder
150 ml (¼ pint) double cream
175 g (6 oz) Greek-style natural yogurt
4 chocolate-coated coffee beans, to decorate

- Chill 4 x 125 ml (4 fl oz) espresso cups or ramekins while you make the filling.

- Melt together the chocolate, espresso powder and 3 tablespoons of the cream in a heatproof bowl set over a saucepan of gently simmering water. Remove from the heat and stir in the remaining cream and half the yogurt.

- Pour into the chilled espresso cups or ramekins. Spoon the remaining yogurt over the top and decorate with a coffee bean. Chill for 10 minutes before serving.

 Chocolate and Coffee Sauce

Melt 200 g (7 oz) plain dark chocolate (75–80% cocoa solids), broken into small pieces, in a heatproof bowl set over a saucepan of gently simmering water. Stir in 100 ml (3½ fl oz) hot strong black coffee, 100 ml (3½ fl oz) whipping cream, 50 g (2 oz) caster sugar and 15 g (½ oz) unsalted butter. Serve immediately poured over ice cream, chocolate brownies or fruit.

 Chocolate and Espresso Slices

Thinly roll out a 375 g (12 oz) pack chilled shortcrust pastry and use to line a 30 x 20 cm (12 x 8 inch) cake tin. Prick the base with a fork, then line with nonstick baking paper and fill with baking beans. Place in a preheated oven, 200°C (400°F), Gas Mark 6, for 10 minutes, then remove the paper and return to the oven for a further 2–3 minutes. Reduce the heat to 180°C (350°F), Gas Mark 4. Meanwhile, melt together 200 g (7 oz) plain dark chocolate (75–80% cocoa solids),

broken into small pieces, and 3 teaspoons espresso powder in a heatproof bowl set over a saucepan of gently simmering water. Place 2 large eggs and 50 g (2 oz) soft light brown sugar in a bowl and beat with a hand-held electric whisk until pale and fluffy, then whisk in the melted chocolate and 100 ml (3½ fl oz) double cream. Fold in 25 g (1 oz) self-raising flour and pour into the pastry case. Return to the oven and cook for 10 minutes. Leave to cool slightly, then dust with cocoa powder and serve warm, cut into 8 slices, with dollops of crème fraîche.

Blueberry Baskets with White Chocolate Sauce

Serves 4

200 g (7 oz) white chocolate (30% cocoa solids), broken into small pieces

4 brandy snap baskets

125 ml (4 fl oz) crème fraîche

1 piece of stem ginger in syrup, finely chopped

1 tablespoon stem ginger syrup (taken from the jar)

450 g (14½ oz) frozen blueberries

- Melt 50 g (2 oz) of the white chocolate in a heatproof bowl set over a saucepan of gently simmering water. Spoon a little into each brandy snap basket, covering the base and sides (this will prevent the sauce running out). Chill for 5 minutes.

- Meanwhile, melt the remaining chocolate, crème fraîche, stem ginger and stem ginger syrup in a saucepan over a low heat, stirring occasionally, until the ingredients have combined.

- Place the baskets on a plate and fill with the blueberries. Pour over the sauce and serve immediately.

White Chocolate and Blueberry Baskets Melt together 100 g (3½ oz) white chocolate (30% cocoa solids), broken into small pieces, and 100 ml (3½ fl oz) double cream in a heatproof bowl set over a saucepan of gently simmering water. Leave to cool slightly, then stir in 100 ml (3½ fl oz) crème fraîche. Spoon the mixture into 4 brandy snap baskets. Chill for 10 minutes, then top with 100 g (3½ oz) blueberries or raspberries.

Blueberry and White Chocolate Pudding Melt 125 g (4 oz) white chocolate (30% cocoa solids), broken into small pieces, in a heatproof bowl set over a saucepan of gently simmering water. Place 50 g (2 oz) softened unsalted butter and 50 g (2 oz) caster sugar in a large bowl and beat with a hand-held electric whisk until light and fluffy. Whisk in 1 large egg, ½ teaspoon vanilla extract and the melted chocolate. Fold in 25 g (1 oz) white chocolate chunks, 75 g (3 oz) self-raising flour and 75 g (3 oz) blueberries. Spoon into an 18 cm (7 inch) round cake tin lined with nonstick baking paper and place in a preheated oven, 180°C (350°F), Gas Mark 4, for 20 minutes. Serve cut into wedges.

Sour Cherry Chocolate Brownie Puddings

Serves 4

75 g (3 oz) unsalted butter,
  softened, plus extra
  for greasing
100 g (3½ oz) soft light
  brown sugar
1 teaspoon vanilla extract
25 g (1 oz) cocoa powder, sifted
50 g (2 oz) self-raising flour, sifted
1 egg
50 g (2 oz) dried sour cherries
double cream or crème fraîche,
  to serve

- Lightly grease 4 holes of a 6-hole nonstick muffin tin. Place the butter, sugar and vanilla extract in a bowl and beat with a hand-held electric whisk until light and fluffy.

- Add the cocoa powder, flour and egg and whisk until combined, then stir in the sour cherries.

- Spoon the mixture into the prepared muffin tin and place in a preheated oven, 180°C (350°F), Gas Mark 4, for 10–12 minutes or until just cooked but still soft in the centres.

- Turn out the puddings on to serving plates and serve immediately with double cream or crème fraîche.

---

10 Chocolate Brownie, Sour Cherry and Ice Cream Sandwiches

Cut 4 shop-bought chocolate brownies in half crossways. Place a scoop of vanilla ice cream in the centre of 1 half, then place another brownie half on top, pressing down gently. Place in the freezer. Repeat to make 4 ice cream sandwiches. Meanwhile, roughly chop 75 g (3 oz) dried sour cherries and place in a saucepan with 200 ml (7 fl oz) shop-bought Belgian chocolate sauce. Warm through and pour over the brownies.

30 Chocolate and Sour Cherry Florentines

Melt 65 g (2½ oz) unsalted butter in a saucepan, add 50 g (2 oz) caster sugar and heat gently until the sugar has dissolved. Bring to the boil, then remove from the heat and stir in 2 tablespoons double cream, 25 g (1 oz) chopped mixed peel, 50 g (2 oz) dried sour cherries, 50 g (2 oz) flaked almonds, 25 g (1 oz) chopped crystallized stem ginger and 15 g (½ oz) plain flour. Place heaped teaspoons of the mixture on to 2 greased nonstick baking sheets, spacing them well apart, and bake one tray at a time in a preheated oven, 180°C (350°F), Gas Mark 4, for 8–10 minutes or until golden brown. Leave on the baking sheets for 2 minutes, then transfer to a wire rack. Dip the edges of the biscuits in 125 g (4 oz) melted plain dark chocolate. Chill in the refrigerator for 10 minutes until set. Serve with chocolate ice cream.

20 Chocolate Blinis

Serves 6

100 g (3½ oz) self-raising flour
15 g (½ oz) cocoa powder
½ teaspoon baking powder
1 tablespoon caster sugar
1 egg, beaten
170 ml (5½ fl oz) milk
1 tablespoon sunflower oil,
   for frying
50 g (2 oz) milk chocolate,
   finely chopped

To serve

100 ml (3½ fl oz) crème fraîche
150 g (5 oz) raspberries

- Sift the flour, cocoa powder and baking powder into a large bowl and stir in the sugar. Make a well in the centre and gradually whisk in the egg and a little of the milk to form a thick batter. Stir in the remaining milk.

- Heat a large nonstick frying pan over a medium heat. Using a scrunched up piece of kitchen paper, dip into the oil and use to wipe over the pan. Drop dessertspoons of the batter into the pan, spacing them well apart.

- Cook for 1 minute, then scatter a little of the chopped chocolate over each. Cook for a further 1–2 minutes until bubbles start to appear on the surface and pop, then flip over and cook for a further 1–2 minutes until just firm. Remove from the pan and keep warm.

- Repeat with the remaining batter to make about 28 blinis, adding more oil if necessary. Serve warm, topped with crème fraîche and raspberries.

 Quick Blinis with Chocolate Sauce
Warm through 24 ready-made blinis according to the packet instructions. Divide between 6 serving dishes, then top each serving with 50 g (2 oz) raspberries. Gently warm through 200 ml (7 fl oz) shop-bought Belgian chocolate sauce in a saucepan, pour over the blinis and serve 4 blinis per person.

Chocolate Blinis with White Chocolate Ganache To make the ganache, melt 150 g (5 oz) white chocolate, broken into small pieces, in a heatproof bowl set over a saucepan of gently simmering water. Remove from the heat and stir in 300 ml (½ pint) crème fraiche and 1 tablespoon white crème de cacao, then chill until slightly thickened. Meanwhile, make the blinis as above and leave to cool. Place a spoonful of the chilled ganache on to each blini and top with a raspberry. Dust with a little cocoa powder and serve immediately as dessert canapés.

 Chocolate Orange
Fondant Puddings

Serves 6

75 g (3 oz) unsalted butter,
  softened, plus extra
  for greasing
300 g (10 oz) plain dark chocolate
  (70% cocoa solids), chopped
grated rind of 1 orange
75 g (3 oz) soft light brown sugar
5 eggs
50 g (2 oz) plain flour, sifted
1 tablespoon orange liqueur
vanilla ice cream or crème
  fraîche, to serve

- Grease 6 x 150 ml (¼ pint) metal pudding moulds or ramekins and place on a baking sheet. Melt the chocolate in a heatproof bowl set over a saucepan of gently simmering water, then add the orange rind, reserving a few strands for decoration. Once the chocolate has melted, stir until smooth, then leave to cool slightly.

- Place the butter, sugar, eggs, flour and liqueur in a food processor or blender and blend to form a smooth batter. Add the melted chocolate and whizz again until well combined.

- Pour the batter into the prepared dishes and place in a preheated oven, 190°C (375°F), Gas Mark 5, for 9 minutes. The outside should be cooked with a molten centre. Serve immediately with scoops of vanilla ice cream or crème fraîche and decorate with the reserved orange rind.

 **Chocolate Orange
Liqueur Sauce**

Place 200 g (7 oz) plain dark chocolate, broken into small pieces, in a heatproof bowl, then pour over 125 ml (4 fl oz) warmed single cream. Stir until the chocolate has melted, then stir in 1 tablespoon orange liqueur. Serve the warm sauce poured over vanilla ice cream.

**Chocolate
Orange Tart**

Melt 200 g (7 oz) plain dark chocolate (85% cocoa solids), broken into small pieces, in a heatproof bowl set over a saucepan of gently simmering water, stirring occasionally, then leave to cool slightly. Meanwhile, place 2 large eggs, 50 g (2 oz) caster sugar and the grated rind of 1 orange in a bowl and beat with a hand-held electric whisk until pale and fluffy. Whisk in the chocolate and 1 tablespoon orange liqueur until well

combined, then stir in 100 ml (3½ fl oz) double cream. Place a 20 cm (8 inch) shop-bought sweet pastry case on a baking sheet. Pour in the chocolate mixture and spread the top level. Place in a preheated oven, 160°C (325°F), Gas Mark 3, for about 10–12 minutes or until just set. The mixture should be slightly wobbly in the centre, but will continue to set on cooling. Leave to cool for 10 minutes, then serve warm with spoonfuls of crème fraîche.

Chocolate Risotto

Serves 4

600 ml (1 pint) milk
2 tablespoons caster sugar
grated rind of 1 orange
25 g (1 oz) unsalted butter
125 g (4 oz) arborio rice
125 g (4 oz) plain dark chocolate,
  chopped into small pieces
1–2 tablespoons of brandy
  or orange liqueur (optional)
25 g (1 oz) toasted hazelnuts,
  chopped, to serve

- Place the milk and sugar in a saucepan and bring to a simmer, along with the majority of the orange rind (reserve a few pieces for decoration).

- Meanwhile, melt the butter in a heavy-based saucepan, add the rice and stir to coat the grains. Add a ladleful of the hot milk and stir well. Once most of the milk has been absorbed, add another ladleful.

- Continue until most of the milk has been absorbed and the rice is creamy but slightly al dente – this should take about 15 minutes.

- Stir in most of the chopped chocolate and brandy or orange liqueur, if using. Spoon into 4 bowls and serve immediately, sprinkled with the hazelnuts and a little grated orange rind.

Quick Chocolate and Orange Rice Pudding Place 2 x 425 g (14 oz) cans rice pudding in a saucepan, then stir in the grated rind of ½ orange, 2 tablespoons orange juice and 100 g (3½ oz) chopped plain dark chocolate. Heat through, stirring, until the chocolate has melted. Spoon into 4 bowls and serve immediately.

 Chocolate Risotto with Pistachio Thins Place 75 g (3 oz) softened unsalted butter and 125 g (4 oz) caster sugar in a bowl and beat with a hand-held electric whisk until light and fluffy. Fold in 50 g (2 oz) sifted plain flour, then stir in 2 tablespoons milk and 75 g (3 oz) chopped pistachio nuts. Place 8 teaspoons of the mixture, placed well apart, on to 2 large baking sheets lined with nonstick baking paper. Place in a preheated oven, 200°C (400°F), Gas Mark 6, for 5–7 minutes or until golden around the edges. Leave to firm up slightly, then lift off using a palette knife and curl around a rolling pin. Transfer to a wire rack to cool. Make the risotto as above and serve with the pistachio thins.

2 Pear and Chocolate Crumbles

Serves 4

butter, for greasing
2 x 410 g (13 oz) cans pear
   quarters in juice, drained
50 g (2 oz) soft light brown sugar
grated rind and juice of
   1 unwaxed lemon
50 g (2 oz) milk chocolate chips
   or chunks
ice cream, to serve (optional)

For the topping

100 g (3½ oz) plain flour
50 g (2 oz) unsalted butter, diced
50 g (2 oz) soft light brown sugar
50 g (2 oz) milk chocolate chips
   or chunks
50 g (2 oz) toasted hazelnuts,
   chopped

- Grease 4 x 300 ml (½ pint) ovenproof dishes or ramekins and place on a baking sheet. Place the pears, sugar, lemon rind and juice and chocolate in a large bowl and stir together.

- To make the topping, place the flour in a bowl, add the butter and rub in with the fingertips until the mixture resembles fine breadcrumbs. Alternatively, use a food processor. Stir in the sugar, chocolate and hazelnuts.

- Spoon the pear mixture into the prepared dishes or ramekins, spooning over any juice. Sprinkle over the topping and press down lightly.

- Place in a preheated oven, 180°C (350°F), Gas Mark 4, for 15 minutes or until golden and bubbling. Serve with spoonfuls of ice cream, if using.

 Pears in Hot Chocolate Sauce

Peel, halve and core 4 ripe pears, then cut each half into slices. Arrange in 4 serving dishes and sprinkle over the juice of 1 lemon. To make the chocolate sauce, place 125 g (4 oz) plain dark chocolate, broken into small pieces, 25 g (1 oz) unsalted butter, 2 tablespoons golden syrup, 2 tablespoons double cream and 3 tablespoons water in a saucepan. Heat gently, stirring until smooth. Spoon over the pears, sprinkle with 25 g (1 oz) chopped toasted hazelnuts and serve immediately.

 **Rosemary Poached Pears with Chocolate Sauce**

Place 300 ml (½ pint) water, 150 g (5 oz) caster sugar and 3 rosemary sprigs in a saucepan and heat gently until the sugar has dissolved, then bring to the boil. Peel 4 pears, then place the whole pears in the syrup. Cover and simmer for 20–25 minutes until tender, turning the pears occasionally. Remove the pears and place in a serving bowl. Boil the syrup for 2 minutes until thick. Place 200 g (7 oz) plain dark chocolate, broken into small pieces, in a heatproof bowl and pour over 150 ml (¼ pint) warmed double cream. Stir until melted. Serve the pears with the strained syrup and sauce.

2 Banana and Chilli Chocolate Chimichangas

Serves 6

2 tablespoons caster sugar

1 teaspoon ground cinnamon

6 ripe bananas, thickly sliced

6 soft tortilla wraps

150 g (5 oz) chilli-flavoured plain dark chocolate, roughly chopped

2 tablespoons sunflower oil

vanilla ice cream, to serve (optional)

- Mix together the sugar and cinnamon in a small bowl.

- Place some of the banana slices in the centre of 1 tortilla, then sprinkle over 25 g (1 oz) of the chocolate. Fold over the edges of the tortilla to meet in the middle. Then roll over, from the side nearest to you. Place fold side down on a baking sheet. Brush with a little oil, then sprinkle over the cinnamon sugar. Repeat with the remaining ingredients to make 6 chimichangas.

- Place in a preheated oven, 190°C (350°F), Gas Mark 5, for 10 minutes or until golden. Serve immediately with scoops of vanilla ice cream, if using.

---

1 Mexican Chocolate and Chilli Fondue

Place 150 ml (¼ pint) double cream in a saucepan and heat gently. Stir in 225 g (7½ oz) chopped plain dark chocolate, 1 deseeded and chopped red chilli and ½ teaspoon chilli powder. Stir over a low heat until the chocolate has melted. Pour into a warm dish and serve with sliced bananas and warm tortilla strips.

3 Warm Chilli Chocolate Pudding

Place 150 g (5 oz) chilli-flavoured plain dark chocolate, 25 g (1 oz) butter and 3 tablespoons golden syrup in a saucepan and cook over a gentle heat, stirring occasionally, until melted, then stir in 3 tablespoons double cream. Pour into a lightly greased 1 litre (1¾ pint) ovenproof dish. Place 125 g (4 oz) softened unsalted butter and 125 g (4 oz) caster sugar in a bowl and beat together with a hand-held electric whisk until light and fluffy. Gradually beat in 2 eggs, then fold in 100 g (3 ½ oz) sifted self-raising flour, 25 g (1 oz) sifted cocoa powder, 1 teaspoon dried chilli flakes and 2 tablespoons milk. Spoon the mixture over the sauce and place in a preheated oven, 180°C (350°F), Gas Mark 4, for 18–20 minutes.

30 Chocolate Pancakes

Serves 4

100 g (3½ oz) plain flour
1 tablespoon cocoa powder
pinch of salt
2 eggs, beaten
300 ml (½ pint) milk
2 tablespoons melted
  unsalted butter
knob of unsalted butter,
  for frying
225 g (7½ oz) shop-bought
  red fruit compote

For the chocolate sauce

175 g (6 oz) milk chocolate,
  broken into small pieces
50 g (2 oz) unsalted butter
2 tablespoons golden syrup
100 ml (3½ fl oz) milk

- Sift the flour, cocoa powder and salt into a large bowl and make a well in the centre. Pour the eggs into the well, then gradually whisk into the flour mixture. Add the milk a little at a time, whisking to form a smooth batter. Stir in the melted butter.

- To make the chocolate sauce, gently melt the chocolate, butter and golden syrup in a saucepan over a low heat. Stir in the milk and cook for 2–3 minutes until the sauce thickens, stirring frequently.

- Heat a little of the butter for frying in a 20 cm (8 inch) nonstick crêpe or frying pan. Add a ladleful of batter and swirl around to coat the bottom of the pan. Cook for 1–2 minutes until golden, then flip over and cook for a further 1 minute. Remove from the pan and keep warm. Repeat with the remaining batter to make 8 pancakes, adding more butter if necessary.

- To serve, fill each pancake with a little of the compote and drizzle with the chocolate sauce. Serve 2 per person.

10 Pancakes with Praline Chocolate

Sauce Melt 200 g (7 oz) Swiss plain dark chocolate with honey and praline nougat, finely chopped, in a heatproof bowl set over a saucepan of gently simmering water until completely soft. Do not overstir. Add 25 g (1 oz) unsalted butter and stir until melted, then stir in 100 ml (3½ fl oz) whipping cream. Meanwhile, heat through 8 ready-made pancakes according to the packet instructions and serve 2 per person drizzled with the chocolate sauce.

20 Chocolate and Raspberry Clafoutis

Place 100 g (3½ oz) softened unsalted butter, 125 g (4 oz) caster sugar, 100 g (3½ oz) self-raising flour, 25 g (1 oz) sifted cocoa powder, 3 eggs and 3 tablespoons milk in a food processor or blender and blend until smooth. Spoon the mixture into 4 x 250 ml (8 fl oz) greased ovenproof dishes, then divide 125 g (4 oz) raspberries between them. Place on a baking sheet and bake in a preheated oven, 190°C (375°F), Gas Mark 5, for 15–16 minutes until risen and set.

3 White Chocolate, Lemon Grass and Cardamom Mousse

Serves 6

100 ml (3½ fl oz) milk
2 lemon grass stalks,
   roughly chopped
250 g (8 oz) white chocolate
   (30% cocoa solids), broken into
   small pieces
crushed seeds from 4 green
   cardamom pods
200 g (7 oz) mascarpone cheese
3 egg whites
white chocolate curls, to serve
cocoa powder, for dusting

- Place 6 small ramekins in a freezer. Pour the milk into a small saucepan and add the lemon grass. Bring to the boil, then remove from the heat and leave to stand and infuse for 5 minutes.

- Meanwhile, melt together the chocolate and crushed cardamom seeds in a heatproof bowl set over a saucepan of gently simmering water, stirring occasionally. Remove from the heat.

- Strain the warm milk into the melted chocolate and stir well. Beat in the mascarpone with a hand-held electric whisk until smooth, then chill.

- Whisk the egg whites in a clean bowl with a hand-held electric whisk until stiff, then gently fold into the chocolate mixture. Spoon into the ramekins and place in the freezer for 5–10 minutes before serving. Alternatively, to make ahead, cover and chill in the refrigerator until required.

- Top with white chocolate curls and dust with cocoa powder and serve.

1 White Chocolate, Lemon Grass and Cardamom Sauce

Place 2 chopped lemon grass stalks, 4 crushed cardamom pods and 100 ml (3½ fl oz) milk in a saucepan and bring to the boil, then remove from the heat and leave to infuse for 5 minutes. Meanwhile, melt 250 g (8 oz) white chocolate, broken into small pieces, in a heatproof bowl set over a saucepan of simmering water, then strain over the milk and stir. Pour over ice cream or fruit.

2 White Chocolate, Lemon Grass and Cardamom Tart

Place 2 chopped lemon grass stalks and 100 ml (3½ fl oz) milk in a saucepan and bring to the boil. Remove from the heat and leave to infuse for 5 minutes. Meanwhile melt 200 g (7 oz) white chocolate (30% cocoa solids) in a heatproof bowl set over a pan of gently simmering water, stirring occasionally. Strain the warm milk into the chocolate and add the crushed seeds of 4 green cardamom pods. Beat together 500 g (1 lb) mascarpone cheese and 25 g (1 oz) icing sugar, then whisk in the chocolate mixture. Spoon the filling into a 20 cm (8 inch) shop-bought sweet pastry case. Chill until ready to serve.

3⦿ Chocolate Sorbet Bites

Serves 4

250 g (8 oz) frozen mango or
   raspberry sorbet
150 g (5 oz) plain dark chocolate,
   broken into small pieces

To decorate (optional)

chopped nuts
dried raspberry flakes
chocolate sprinkles

- Line a large baking sheet with nonstick baking paper and place in the freezer, set on its lowest setting, for 5 minutes.

- Using a melon baller, shape the sorbet into about 16 balls and place on the baking sheet. Insert a cocktail stick into each ball, then place in the freezer.

- Melt the chocolate in a heatproof bowl set over a saucepan of gently simmering water, stirring occasionally. Leave to cool to room temperature. One by one dip the sorbet balls into the chocolate so they are completely coated.

- Decorate, if liked, with chopped nuts, raspberry flakes and chocolate sprinkles and return to the freezer for at least 10 minutes.

- Remove from the freezer 5 minutes before serving.

 Ice Cream Wafer Choc Ices

Melt 50 g (2 oz) plain dark chocolate, broken into small pieces, in a heatproof bowl set over a saucepan of gently simmering water. Brush the melted chocolate on to one side of 8 ice cream wafers. Cut 4 thick slices of ice cream, taken from a block the same size as the wafer, and place on the chocolate sides of 4 wafers. Sandwich together with the remaining wafers, chocolate side down, and serve immediately.

 Chocolate Cornets

Melt 175 g (6 oz) plain dark chocolate, broken into small pieces, in a heatproof bowl set over a saucepan of gently simmering water. Dip the ends of 4 waffle cones into the melted chocolate, then stand in glasses and pour the remaining chocolate into the bottom of each cone. Chill for 10 minutes until set. Add a little chopped fresh fruit to the bottom of the cones, then top with sorbet or ice cream. Serve immediately.

30 White Chocolate and Strawberry Cheesecake

Serves 6–8

150 g (5 oz) digestive biscuits, crushed

75 g (3 oz) unsalted butter, melted

200 g (7 oz) white chocolate (30% cocoa solids), broken into small pieces

500 g (1 lb) mascarpone cheese

25 g (1 oz) icing sugar, sifted

200 g (7 oz) strawberries, hulled and sliced

grated white chocolate, to decorate

- Stir the crushed biscuits into the melted butter and press into the base of a 20 cm (8 inch) loose-bottomed round cake tin. Chill while you make the filling.

- Melt the chocolate in a heatproof bowl set over a saucepan of gently simmering water, stirring occasionally.

- Place the mascarpone in a bowl and whisk in the icing sugar until smooth. Whisk in the chocolate, then spread the mixture over the cheesecake base.

- Chill for 15 minutes, then arrange the strawberries over the top and decorate with the grated chocolate. Serve immediately or chill until ready to serve.

1 Strawberries with Warm White Chocolate Sauce

Hull and halve 650 g (1 lb 5 oz) strawberries and divide between 6 glasses. Warm 400 ml (14 fl oz) double cream in a small saucepan. Remove from the heat and stir in 175 g (6 oz) chopped white chocolate. Stir until melted, then pour over the strawberries. Serve immediately.

2 Individual White Chocolate and Strawberry Cheesecakes

Divide 6 crushed digestive biscuits between 6 small glasses. Place 300 g (10 oz) hulled and chopped strawberries in a bowl and sprinkle with 1 tablespoon icing sugar. Meanwhile, melt 125 g (4 oz) white chocolate (30% cocoa solids), broken into small pieces, in a heatproof bowl set over a saucepan of gently simmering water, then leave to cool slightly. Place 250 g (8 oz) mascarpone cheese, 125 ml (4 fl oz) double cream and 1 tablespoon icing sugar in a large bowl and beat in the melted chocolate. Spoon into the glasses, then top with the strawberries. Chill until ready to serve.

 # Chocolate and Cherry Trifle

Serves 6–8

75 g (3 oz) plain dark chocolate, broken into small pieces

500 g (1 lb) pot fresh vanilla custard

400 g (13 oz) shop-bought chocolate Swiss roll, cut into 1 cm (½ inch) thick slices

100 g (3½ oz) cherry conserve or jam

4 tablespoons kirsch

450 g (14½ oz) cherries, halved and pitted, plus extra to decorate

450 ml (¾ pint) whipping cream

chocolate curls, to decorate

- Melt the chocolate in a heatproof bowl set over a saucepan of gently simmering water, then leave to cool. Place the custard in a bowl and whisk in the melted chocolate.

- Line the sides and base of a 20 cm (8 inch) trifle bowl with the Swiss roll. Mix together the jam and kirsch in a bowl, then spoon over the sponge. Scatter the cherries over the top and spoon over the chocolate custard.

- Lightly whip the cream in a bowl with a hand-held electric whisk until it forms soft peaks, then spoon over the custard. Decorate with chocolate curls and a few extra cherries. Serve immediately or chill until ready to serve.

 Quick Chocolate Cherry Puddings

Cut a shop-bought chocolate Swiss roll into 6 x 1.5 cm (¾ inch) thick slices and place in 6 bowls. Spoon 1 tablespoon kirsch, taken from a jar of cherries in kirsch, over each, then spoon 4 of the cherries from the jar into each bowl. Place 450 g (14½ oz) shop-bought fresh vanilla custard in a saucepan and heat gently, then stir in 50 g (2 oz) chopped plain dark chocolate and stir until melted. Serve poured over the puddings.

 Chocolate and Cherry Tart

Place 150 g (5 oz) soft cream cheese, 125 ml (4 fl oz) double cream, 2 tablespoons sifted cocoa powder, 3 tablespoons caster sugar and 2 egg yolks in a bowl and beat together. Spoon into a 20 cm (8 inch) shop-bought sweet pastry case. Drain a 425 g (14 oz) can pitted black cherries and arrange over the chocolate mixture. Place in a preheated oven, 180°C (350°F), Gas Mark 4, for 18–20 minutes or until set.

Spiced Chocolate Sponge with Belgian Chocolate Sauce

Serves 4–6

125 g (4 oz) unsalted butter, cut into pieces, plus extra for greasing

200 ml (7 fl oz) shop-bought Belgian chocolate sauce

125 g (4 oz) plain dark chocolate, broken into small pieces

125 g (4 oz) soft light brown sugar

125 g (4 oz) self-raising flour

1 teaspoon ground cinnamon

½ teaspoon ground nutmeg

¼ teaspoon ground cloves

2 eggs, beaten

2 tablespoons milk

single cream, to serve (optional)

- Lightly grease a 1 litre (1¾ pint) ovenproof dish, then pour the Belgian chocolate sauce in the bottom.

- Melt together the butter and chocolate in a heatproof bowl set over a saucepan of gently simmering water, then stir in the sugar.

- Sift the flour and spices into a large bowl, then pour in the chocolate mixture, eggs and milk and mix well.

- Spoon the mixture over the sauce (if it sinks, don't worry; it will rise on cooking) and place in a preheated oven, 180°C (350°F), Gas Mark 4, for 20–25 minutes or until risen and bubbling.

- Leave to cool in the dish for a few minutes, then serve with single cream, if using.

---

1 **Quick Spiced Chocolate Sauce**

Gently warm through 200 ml (7 fl oz) shop-bought Belgian chocolate sauce in a saucepan and stir in 1 teaspoon ground cinnamon and ¼ teaspoon each of ground cloves and nutmeg. Serve poured over vanilla ice cream.

2 **Individual Spiced Melting Chocolate Puddings** Melt together 175 g (6 oz) plain dark chocolate (70% cocoa solids), broken into small pieces, and 175 g (6 oz) diced unsalted butter in a heatproof bowl set over a saucepan of gently simmering water, stirring occasionally. Place 3 eggs, plus 3 egg yolks and 6 tablespoons caster sugar, in a bowl and beat with a hand-held electric whisk until thick and foamy. Whisk in the melted chocolate, then sift in 3 heaped teaspoons plain flour, ½ teaspoon ground cinnamon and ¼ teaspoon each ground cloves and nutmeg. Spoon the mixture into 6 x 175 ml (6 fl oz) greased ramekins or metal pudding moulds, their bases lined with nonstick baking paper. Place on a baking sheet and bake in a preheated oven, 220°C (425°F), Gas Mark 7, for 10 minutes or until set but still soft in the centres. Turn out the puddings on to serving plates and serve immediately.

3 Chocolate and Ginger Tart

Serves 6–8

200 g (7 oz) plain dark chocolate (85% cocoa solids), broken into small pieces
2 large eggs
50 g (2 oz) caster sugar
2 pieces of stem ginger in syrup, finely chopped
100 ml (3½ fl oz) double cream
20 cm (8 inch) shop-bought sweet pastry case
cocoa powder, for dusting
vanilla ice cream or crème fraîche, to serve (optional)

- Melt the chocolate in a heatproof bowl set over a saucepan of gently simmering water, stirring occasionally, then leave to cool slightly.

- Place the eggs and sugar in a bowl and beat with a hand-held electric whisk until pale and fluffy. Whisk in the melted chocolate until well combined, then stir in the stem ginger and cream.

- Place the pastry case on a baking sheet. Pour in the chocolate mixture and spread the top level. Place in a preheated oven, 160°C (325° F), Gas Mark 3, for about 10–12 minutes or until just set. The mixture should be slightly wobbly in the centre, but will continue to set on cooling.

- Dust with cocoa powder. Serve warm or cold with a scoop of vanilla ice cream or crème frâiche, if using.

1 Chocolate and Ginger Sauce

Melt together 200 g (7 oz) plain dark chocolate, broken into small pieces, 300 ml (½ pint) double cream, 2 pieces of stem ginger in syrup, finely chopped, and 2 tablespoons stem ginger syrup in a saucepan over a low heat. Cook until melted and smooth and shiny, stirring occasionally. The sauce is delicious poured over vanilla ice cream or bananas.

2 Chocolate and Ginger Mousses

Melt together 150 g (5 oz) plain dark chocolate, broken into small pieces, and 2 pieces of stem ginger in syrup, finely chopped, in a heatproof bowl set over a saucepan of gently simmering water. Meanwhile, whip 125 ml (4 fl oz) double cream in a bowl using a hand-held electric whisk until it forms soft peaks. Fold the chocolate mixture, a little at a time, into the cream. Whisk 2 egg whites in a clean bowl with a hand-held electric whisk until stiff, then gently fold into the chocolate cream. Spoon into 6 small espresso cups or ramekins and chill for 10 minutes.

30 Chocolate and Pistachio Soufflés

Serves 6

butter, for greasing
25 g (1 oz) pistachio nuts, ground
150 g (5 oz) plain dark chocolate
  (72% cocoa solids), broken into
  small pieces
4 eggs, separated
100 g (3½ oz) caster sugar
2 teaspoons cornflour
cocoa powder or icing sugar,
  for dusting (optional)

- Grease 6 x 175 ml (6 fl oz) ramekins, then lightly dust with 1 tablespoon of the ground pistachios to cover the base and sides. (This helps the soufflés to rise.) Place on a baking sheet.

- Melt the chocolate in a heatproof bowl set over a saucepan of gently simmering water, then leave to cool slightly.

- Meanwhile, whisk the egg whites in a clean large bowl with a hand-held electric whisk until stiff, then gradually whisk in half the sugar until the mixture is thick and glossy.

- Stir the remaining sugar, egg yolks and cornflour into the cooled chocolate mixture. Gently fold some of the egg white mixture into the chocolate mixture, then gently fold in the remainder, with the remaining pistachios. Spoon into the prepared dishes and spread the tops level, then clean the edges with a fingertip.

- Place in a preheated oven, 190°C (375°F), Gas Mark 5, for 20 minutes or until risen. Dust with cocoa powder or icing sugar, if using, and serve immediately.

1 Pistachio and Choc Chip Freeze

Place 600 g (1 lb 3½ oz) pistachio ice cream and 125 g (4 oz) milk chocolate chips in a food processor and pulse until just combined. Spoon into 6 small glasses. Scatter over 25 g (1 oz) chopped pistachios and serve immediately with ice cream wafers.

2 Pistachio Chocolate Brownie Puddings

Place 75 g (3 oz) softened unsalted butter, 100 g (3½ oz) soft light brown sugar and 1 teaspoon vanilla extract in a bowl and beat with a hand-held electric whisk until light and fluffy. Add 25 g (1 oz) sifted cocoa powder, 50 g (2 oz) self-raising flour and 1 egg and whisk until combined. Stir in 50 g (2 oz) roughly chopped pistachios. Spoon the mixture into a lightly greased 6-hole nonstick muffin tin and place in a preheated oven, 180°C (350°F), Gas Mark 4, for 10–12 minutes or until just cooked but still soft in the centres. Turn out the puddings on to serving plates and serve immediately with double cream or crème fraîche.

30 Apricot, Chocolate and Brioche Tart

Serves 6–8

butter, for greasing

225 g (7½ oz) brioche loaf, cut into 1 cm (½ inch) slices

100 g (3½ oz) milk or plain dark chocolate drops or chunks

1 large egg

25 g (1 oz) caster sugar

250 g (8 oz) mascarpone cheese

2 x 410 g (13 oz) cans apricot halves, drained

3 tablespoons demerara sugar

- Lightly grease a shallow rectangular tart tin, about 30 x 20 cm (12 x 8 inch). Arrange the brioche slices in the bottom, cutting them to fit where necessary and filling any gaps with the bread. Scatter over half the chocolate.

- Lightly whisk together the egg, caster sugar and mascarpone in a bowl until smooth, then spoon over the bread, leaving a 1 cm (½ inch) border. Scatter over the remaining chocolate.

- Arrange the apricots in neat lines, cut side up, over the mascarpone mixture and sprinkle with the demerara sugar.

- Place in a preheated oven, 180°C (350°F), Gas Mark 4, for 20–25 minutes or until the custard is set. Serve in slices.

 1 Apricot Brioche Toasts with Chocolate Sauce Lightly toast 6 thick slices of brioche, place on 6 serving plates and top each with 1 apricot, halved and stoned. Meanwhile, melt 150 g (5 oz) plain dark chocolate, broken into small pieces, 2 tablespoons orange liqueur and 4 tablespoons double cream in a heatproof bowl set over a saucepan of gently simmering water. Pour over the apricot toasts and serve immediately.

 2 Chocolate Brioche with Sticky Apricots Beat together 2 eggs, 200 ml (7 fl oz) milk and 2 tablespoons caster sugar in a shallow dish. Add 6 slices of chocolate brioche, each cut in half, and turn to coat. Melt together 25 g (1 oz) unsalted butter and 2 tablespoons caster sugar in a frying pan, add 450 g (14½ oz) halved and stoned apricots and cook gently for 5 minutes until the apricots have softened and released their juice. Melt 25 g (1 oz) unsalted butter in a large frying pan and add the brioche. Cook for 2 minutes on each side or until golden brown, then serve 2 slices per person topped with the apricots and their juice and a scoop of vanilla ice cream.

30 Fruity Chocolate Bread and Butter Pudding

Serves 4

25 g (1 oz) unsalted butter,
softened, plus extra
for greasing

100 g (3½ oz) milk chocolate,
broken into small pieces

12 slices of fruit loaf

500 g (1 lb) pot fresh custard

100 ml (3½ fl oz) milk

25 g (1 oz) sultanas

2 tablespoons demerara sugar

- Grease a 1 litre (1¾ pint) ovenproof dish. Melt the chocolate in a heatproof bowl set over a saucepan of gently simmering water. Meanwhile, butter each slice of bread, then cut in half diagonally, forming triangles.

- Place the custard in a jug and stir in the melted chocolate. Make up the custard to 600 g (1 lb 3½ oz) with the milk.

- Arrange a layer of bread in the bottom of the prepared dish. Sprinkle with the sultanas, then place the remaining bread on top. Pour over the chocolate custard and leave to stand for 5 minutes.

- Sprinkle with the sugar and place in a preheated oven, 180°C (350°F), Gas Mark 4, for 20 minutes or until bubbling.

---

1 Fruity Chocolate Cinnamon Bread

Beat together 2 large eggs and 3 tablespoons milk in a shallow dish. Spread 2 slices of fruit bread with 2 tablespoons chocolate spread, then place another 2 slices of bread on top. Add to the egg mixture and leave for 1 minute, then turn to coat. Melt a knob of unsalted butter and 1 tablespoon oil in a large frying pan and cook the eggy breads on each side for 3–4 minutes until puffed and golden. Cut in half, place on 4 serving plates and serve sprinkled with 2 tablespoons caster sugar mixed with 1 teaspoon ground cinnamon.

2 Individual Chocolate and Orange Bread Puddings

Spread 12 slices of fruit bread with 25 g (1 oz) softened unsalted butter and cut into triangles. Arrange 1 layer of the bread in the bottom of 4 lightly greased 250 ml (8 fl oz) ovenproof dishes. Mix together 500 g (1 lb) pot fresh Belgian chocolate custard with the grated rind of 1 orange and 2 tablespoons orange juice. Pour half over the bread. Repeat until all the ingredients are used up. Sprinkle with 2 tablespoons demerara sugar. Place on a baking sheet and bake in a preheated oven, 180°C (350°F), Gas Mark 4, for 15 minutes or until bubbling.

30 Gooey Chocolate and Prune Torte

Serves 8

150 g (5 oz) plain dark chocolate (70% cocoa solids), broken into small pieces
4 tablespoons brandy
125 g (4 oz) ready-to-eat prunes, roughly chopped
100 g (3½ oz) unsalted butter, diced
4 eggs, separated
100 g (3½ oz) caster sugar
50 g (2 oz) plain flour
1 teaspoon baking powder
whipped cream, to serve
cocoa powder, for dusting

- Base-line a 20 cm (8 inch) round springform cake tin with nonstick baking paper. Melt together the chocolate, brandy, prunes and butter in a heatproof bowl set over a saucepan of gently simmering water.

- Meanwhile, place the egg yolks and sugar in a bowl and whisk with a hand-held electric whisk until pale and thick and the whisk leaves a trail when lifted above the mixture. Fold in the flour and baking powder. Add the melted chocolate mixture, stirring gently to combine.

- Whisk the egg whites in a clean large bowl with a hand-held electric whisk until stiff, then lightly fold into the chocolate mixture.

- Spoon into the prepared tin and place in a preheated oven, 180°C (350°F), Gas Mark 4, for 20 minutes or until risen and set on top, but still soft in the centre. Leave to cool in the tin for a few minutes.

- Place the torte on a serving plate and serve immediately with whipped cream and a dusting of cocoa powder.

 Chocolate-coated Prunes
Melt 175 g (6 oz) plain dark chocolate, broken into small pieces, in a heatproof bowl set over a saucepan of gently simmering water, then remove from the heat. Using a fork, dip 225 g (7½ oz) pitted prunes into the chocolate. Place on a baking sheet lined with nonstick baking paper and chill for 5–8 minutes until set. Serve dusted with cocoa powder and accompanied by coffee.

Chocolate and Prune Refrigerator Bars Melt 250 g (8 oz) plain dark chocolate (at least 70% cocoa solids), broken into small pieces, in a heatproof bowl set over a saucepan of gently simmering water, then stir in 50 g (2 oz) unsalted butter. Using a rolling pin, roughly bash 125 g (4 oz) digestive biscuits into small pieces and stir into the chocolate mixture with 125 g (4 oz) chopped ready-to-eat prunes. Spoon the mixture into a 20 cm (8 inch) square cake tin lined with nonstick baking paper and place in the freezer for 10 minutes to set. Using a sharp knife, cut into 12 bars. Store any leftover bars in an airtight container for up to 3–4 days.

3 Chocolate Mousse with Honeycomb

Serves 6

200 g (7 oz) plain dark chocolate,
broken into small pieces
4 eggs, separated
150 ml (¼ pint) double cream

For the honeycomb

sunflower oil, for greasing
5 tablespoons granulated sugar
2 tablespoons golden syrup
1 teaspoon bicarbonate of soda

- To make the honeycomb, oil a baking sheet and set on a chopping board. Gently heat the sugar and golden syrup in a heavy-based saucepan until the sugar has dissolved, then boil until the mixture turns a deep golden caramel. Whisk in the bicarbonate of soda (this will make it foam up), then quickly pour it on to the prepared baking sheet and leave to cool for 10 minutes.

- Meanwhile, melt the chocolate in a heatproof bowl set over a saucepan of gently simmering water. Leave to cool slightly, then stir in the egg yolks. Lightly whip the cream in a bowl with a hand-held electric whisk until it forms soft peaks and fold into the chocolate mixture.

- Whisk the egg whites in a clean large bowl with a hand-held electric whisk until stiff, then fold into the chocolate cream.

- Break the honeycomb into small chunks and fold most of it into the mousse. Pour into 6 glass tumblers or dishes and chill for 10 minutes until set. Sprinkle the leftover honeycomb over the top just before serving.

---

1 **Easy Crunchy Chocolate Honeycomb Ice Cream** Place 2 large scoops of vanilla ice cream into each of 6 bowls. Roughly break up 2 x 40 g (1¾ oz) bars chocolate honeycomb and sprinkle over the ice cream. Drizzle each with 2 tablespoons warmed shop-bought Belgian chocolate sauce and serve immediately.

2 **Speedy Chocolate and Honeycomb Pots** Melt 150 g (5 oz) milk chocolate, broken into small pieces, in a heatproof bowl set over a saucepan of gently simmering water, then stir in 2 x 40 g (1¾ oz) crumbled chocolate and honeycomb bars. Gently whisk together 300 ml (½ pint) double cream and 250 g (8 oz) mascarpone cheese in a bowl and fold in the chocolate mixture. Spoon into 6 small glasses and chill for 10 minutes. Serve with extra grated chocolate.

QuickCook
Family Favourites

Recipes listed by cooking time

30

20

10

30 Banoffee Pie

Serves 6–8

275 g (9 oz) digestive or ginger biscuits, crushed

100 g (3½ oz) unsalted butter, melted

150 ml (¼ pint) double or whipping cream

3 small bananas

400 g (13 oz) can caramel (dulce de leche)

1 chocolate flake, crumbled

- Stir the crushed biscuits into the melted butter and press into the base and sides of a 19 cm (7½ inch) loose-bottomed fluted flan tin. Chill for 15 minutes.

- Meanwhile, lightly whip the cream in a bowl with a hand-held electric whisk until it forms soft peaks. Slice the bananas.

- Spread the caramel over the biscuit base and top with most of the banana slices, reserving a few for decoration.

- Cover with the whipped cream and decorate with the remaining bananas and crumbled flake. Serve immediately or chill until ready to serve.

---

1 Banoffee Ice Cream Sundaes

Crumble 6 ginger biscuits and place in the bottom of 6 tall sundae glasses. Slice 6 bananas and arrange half over the top of the biscuits. Add 1 scoop of vanilla ice cream to each glass, then drizzle with 2 tablespoons warmed shop-bought toffee sauce. Add the remaining bananas and another scoop of ice cream to each, then top with more toffee sauce. Serve immediately.

2 Banoffee Fools

Crush 8 ginger biscuits and mix with 25 g (1 oz) melted unsalted butter. Slice 3 large bananas and place in a bowl. Sprinkle with 1 tablespoon lemon juice, then stir in 7 tablespoons caramel (dulce de leche). Lightly whip 200 ml (7 fl oz) double cream in a bowl with a hand-held electric whisk until it forms soft peaks, then fold in 300 g (10 oz) shop-bought fresh custard. Spoon 1 tablespoon of the biscuit crumbs into each of 6 tumblers, spoon over half the banoffee mixture and half the custard mixture. Repeat the layers, then top with a little grated chocolate. Serve immediately.

Blueberry Pancakes

Serves 4

150 g (5 oz) plain flour
1 teaspoon baking powder
pinch of salt
2 tablespoons caster sugar
150 ml (¼ pint) milk
25 g (1 oz) unsalted butter,
   melted
1 egg
½ teaspoon vanilla extract
knob of unsalted butter,
   for frying
125 g (4 oz) blueberries

To serve

maple syrup or honey
vanilla ice cream

- Sift the flour, baking powder and salt into a bowl. Stir in the sugar and make a well in the centre. Whisk together the milk, melted butter, egg and vanilla extract in a jug, then gradually whisk into the flour to form a smooth batter.

- Heat a little of the butter for frying in a large frying pan over a medium heat. Add heaped tablespoons of the batter mixture to make pancakes about 8–10 cm (3½–4 inches) in diameter.

- Scatter the blueberries over the top of the batter and cook for 2–3 minutes until bubbles start to appear on the surface, then flip over and cook for a further 1–2 minutes. Remove from the pan and keep warm. Repeat with the remaining batter to make 8–10 pancakes, adding a little more butter to the pan and reducing the heat if necessary.

- Serve the pancakes drizzled with maple syrup or honey, with a scoop of ice cream on top.

Blueberry Compote

Place 200 g (7 oz) blueberries, 2 tablespoons caster sugar and 1 tablespoon lemon juice in a saucepan and heat gently, stirring occasionally, until the blueberries start to pop and release their juice. Simmer for 3–4 minutes until jammy. Delicious served poured over warmed ready-made pancakes or ice cream.

Blueberry Batter Puddings

Sift 75 g (3 oz) plain flour and a pinch of salt into a bowl. Stir in 50 g (2 oz) caster sugar and make a well in the centre. Whisk together 200 ml (7 fl oz) milk, 1 teaspoon vanilla extract and 2 large eggs in a jug, then gradually whisk into the flour to form a smooth batter. Pour into a lightly greased 12-hole bun tray, then scatter 125 g (4 oz) blueberries into the centre of each pudding. Place in a preheated oven, 180°C (350°F), Gas Mark 4, for 20 minutes or until risen, golden and cooked through. Serve 3 puddings per person, dusted with icing sugar.

DES-FAMI-NIO

1 Strawberry Eton Mess

Serves 6

500 g (1 lb) strawberries,
hulled and chopped
2 teaspoons icing sugar
450 ml (¾ pint) double cream
8 meringue nests, broken into
2.5 cm (1 inch) pieces

- Place half the strawberries and the icing sugar in a food processor or blender and blend to form a purée.

- Lightly whip the cream in a large bowl with a hand-held electric whisk until it forms soft peaks, then fold in the meringue nests and remaining strawberries. Swirl in half the purée.

- Spoon into 4 glasses, drizzle with the remaining purée and serve immediately.

 Meringues with Strawberry Cream

Place 150 g (5 oz) hulled strawberries and 1 tablespoon icing sugar in a food processor or blender and blend to form a purée. Lightly whip 200 ml (7 fl oz) double cream in a bowl with a hand-held electric whisk until it forms soft peaks, then stir in the strawberry purée. Spoon into 6 meringue nests and decorate each with a strawberry. Chill for 10 minutes before serving.

 Baked Strawberry Meringue Pie

Roll out 325 g (11 oz) shop-bought chilled shortcrust pastry on a lightly floured surface and use to line a 23 cm (9 inch) loose-bottomed flan tin, then prick the base with a fork. Line with nonstick baking paper and baking beans and bake in a preheated oven, 190°C (375°F), Gas Mark 5, for 10 minutes. Remove the paper and beans and return to the oven for a further 5 minutes or until golden. Spread the base of the pie with 2 tablespoons strawberry jam, then arrange 375 g (12 oz) hulled and halved strawberries over the jam. Whisk 4 egg whites in a clean large bowl with a hand-held electric whisk until stiff, then gradually whisk in 200 g (7 oz) caster sugar until the mixture is thick and glossy. Pile on top of the pie, then place in the oven for 8–10 minutes or until the meringue is golden.

Lemon and Ricotta Pancakes

Serves 4

250 g (8 oz) ricotta cheese
125 ml (4 fl oz) milk
3 eggs, separated
grated rind and juice of
　1 unwaxed lemon
100 g (3½ oz) plain flour
1 teaspoon baking powder
pinch of salt
3 tablespoons caster sugar,
　plus extra for sprinkling
knob of unsalted butter,
　for frying

- Place the ricotta, milk, egg yolks and lemon rind in a large bowl and beat together. Stir in the flour, baking powder, salt and sugar.

- Whisk the egg whites in a clean large bowl with a hand-held electric whisk until stiff, then gently fold into the ricotta mixture.

- Heat a little of the butter in a large frying pan over a medium heat and add heaped dessertspoons of batter to form pancakes about 7 cm (3 inches) in diameter. Cook for 1–2 minutes on each side until golden brown. Remove from the pan and keep warm. Repeat with the remaining batter to make about 24 pancakes, adding a little more butter and reducing the heat if necessary.

- Serve a small stack of pancakes on each of 4 plates, drizzled with the lemon juice and sprinkled with a little caster sugar.

Quick Lemon Pancakes

Warm through 8 ready-made pancakes according to the packet instructions. Sprinkle with caster sugar and lemon juice, to taste, and serve 2 pancakes per person with wedges of lemon.

Pancakes with Lemon Butter

Sift 100 g (3½ oz) plain flour and a pinch of salt into a large bowl and make a well in the centre. Pour 2 beaten eggs into the well, then gradually whisk into the flour. Add 300 ml (½ pint) milk a little at a time, whisking to form a smooth batter. Stir in 2 tablespoons melted unsalted butter. To make the lemon butter, place 125 g (4 oz) unsalted softened butter, 125 g (4 oz) icing sugar and the grated rind of 1 unwaxed lemon in a bowl and beat together with a hand-held electric whisk until light and fluffy. Chill the butter while you make the pancakes. Heat a little unsalted butter in a 20 cm (8 inch) nonstick crêpe or frying pan. Add a ladleful of batter and swirl around to coat the bottom of the pan. Cook for 1–2 minutes until golden, then flip over and cook for a further minute. Repeat with the remaining batter to make 8 pancakes and keep warm. Melt a knob of the lemon butter in the pan and add a little lemon juice. Return a pancake to the foaming butter and heat through. Fold in half and then in quarters. Repeat with the remaining butter and pancakes. Serve 2 pancakes per person on warmed plates.

1 Bananas and Pecans with Butterscotch Custard

Serves 4

100 g (3½ oz) light muscovado
   sugar
2 tablespoons golden syrup
50 g (2 oz) unsalted butter, diced
300 g (10 oz) evaporated milk
2 tablespoons custard powder
2 tablespoons cold water
2 tablespoons rum (optional)
4 large bananas, sliced
50 g (2 oz) chopped pecan nuts

- Place the sugar, golden syrup and butter in a saucepan over a medium heat and bring to the boil, stirring occasionally. Pour in 200 ml (7 fl oz) of the evaporated milk and cook for 3 minutes.

- Place the custard powder in a medium bowl and stir in the measurement water to form a paste, then gradually stir in the remaining evaporated milk until smooth. Pour into the hot sauce and cook, stirring continuously, for 2–3 minutes until the custard is thick and smooth. Stir in the rum, if using.

- Arrange the bananas in a dish and sprinkle over the pecans. Pour over the hot custard and serve immediately.

2 Bananas with Butterscotch

Sauce Melt together 65 g (2½ oz) unsalted butter and 125 g (4 oz) soft dark brown sugar in a large frying pan over a medium heat. Peel 4 bananas and leave whole. Place in the pan and cook for 3–4 minutes on each side. Stir in 2 tablespoons rum (optional) and cook for a further 2–3 minutes. Serve immediately with the sauce and scoops of vanilla ice cream.

3 Banana and Butterscotch

Self-saucing Puddings
Place 125 g (4 oz) self-raising flour and 100 g (3½ oz) caster sugar in a bowl, then whisk in 2 mashed bananas, 1 lightly beaten egg, 2 tablespoons golden syrup, 125 ml (4 fl oz) milk and 85 g (3¼ oz) melted unsalted butter. Stir in 50 g (2 oz) chopped pecans. Pour into 4 greased 450 ml (¾ pint) ovenproof dishes placed on a baking sheet. Place 150 g

(5 oz) soft dark brown sugar, 4 tablespoons golden syrup and 250 ml (8 fl oz) boiling water in a saucepan and bring to the boil, stirring until the sugar has dissolved. Pour into a jug and then pour equally over the puddings. Place in a preheated oven, 180°C (350°F), Gas Mark 4, for 20–25 minutes.

 # Cinnamon Brioche French Toast with Mixed Berries

Serves 4

1 large egg
1 teaspoon ground cinnamon
2 tablespoons caster sugar
125 ml (4 fl oz) milk
knob of unsalted butter, for frying
4 thick slices of brioche bread
375 g (12 oz) mixed berries,
   such as strawberries,
   raspberries, blueberries,
   redcurrants and blackcurrants
vanilla ice cream, to serve

- Mix together the egg, cinnamon and sugar in a shallow dish, then whisk in the milk.

- Heat a large frying pan over a medium heat and add a little butter. Dip 2 slices of the bread in the egg mixture, then place in the hot pan. Cook for 2–3 minutes on each side until golden. Remove from the pan and keep warm. Repeat with the remaining bread, adding a little more butter if necessary.

- Top with the mixed berries and serve with scoops of vanilla ice cream.

2 Cinnamon Brioche French Toast with Summer Fruit Compote

Place 500 g (1 lb) mixed berries, such as raspberries, hulled and halved strawberries and blackcurrants, in a large saucepan with 75 g (3 oz) caster sugar and 2–3 tablespoons water. Bring to the boil and simmer for about 5 minutes, then leave to cool for 10 minutes. Meanwhile, make the brioche toast as above. Serve the cooled compote over the brioche toasts.

3 Brioche Summer Puddings

Make the Summer Fruit Compote (see left). Pour the simmered mixture into a sieve over a bowl, reserving the berries and the juice. Leave to cool for 10 minutes. Cut 8 slices of brioche and lightly toast. Place 4 pieces of the bread on 4 serving plates and spoon over some of the juice, then some of the berries. Top with the remaining brioche slices, pouring over more juice and berries. Serve immediately with thick double cream.

Warm Marshmallow Dip with Fruit Skewers

Serves 4

250 g (8 oz) mixed fruit, such as small strawberries, bananas, cherries and raspberries

250 g (8 oz) pink and white marshmallows

100 ml (3½ fl oz) single cream

- Prepare the fruit if necessary, by hulling the strawberries, slicing the bananas into bite-sized pieces and pitting the cherries. Thread the fruit on to short bamboo skewers.

- Heat the marshmallows and cream in a nonstick saucepan over a low heat, stirring continuously, until the marshmallows have melted. Pour into a warm bowl and serve with the fruit skewers for dipping.

 Marshmallow Brochettes with Chocolate Sauce Melt 50 g (2 oz) plain dark chocolate, broken into small pieces, in a heatproof bowl set over a saucepan of gently simmering water. Whisk in 15 g (½ oz) unsalted butter and 3 tablespoons double cream to form a smooth sauce. Thread 200 g (7 oz) pink and white marshmallows, alternately, on to 8 x 12 cm (5 inch) metal skewers, then run over a gas flame or use a chef's blow torch to singe the edges. Serve 2 brochettes per person with the chocolate sauce.

Marshmallow Mousse Make the Warm Marshmallow Dip as above and chill for 5 minutes. Meanwhile, whisk 2 egg whites in a clean bowl with a hand-held electric whisk until stiff, then gently fold into the marshmallow mixture. Spoon into 4 glasses and chill for 10–15 minutes until set. Serve decorated with mini marshmallows.

Rocky Road Ice Cream Sundaes

Serves 4

8 tablespoons shop-bought
  Belgian chocolate sauce
100 g (3½ oz) chocolate
  chip cookies, broken into
  small pieces
16 small scoops of vanilla
  ice cream
200 g (7 oz) pink and white
  marshmallows

To serve

a few mini marshmallows
a little grated chocolate

- Place the chocolate sauce in a saucepan over a low heat and warm through.

- Meanwhile, place a handful of the biscuits in each of 4 tall sundae glasses. Add 2 scoops of vanilla ice cream to each glass. Add 25 g (1 oz) of the marshmallows to each sundae, then spoon 1 tablespoon of the warm chocolate sauce over each. Repeat the layers, finishing with the chocolate sauce.

- Decorate with a few mini marshmallows and a little grated chocolate. Serve immediately with long spoons.

 Rocky Road Cookies

Place 125 g (4 oz) softened unsalted butter and 125 g (4 oz) soft light brown sugar in a bowl and beat with a hand-held electric whisk until light and fluffy. Whisk in 1 beaten egg and 1 tablespoon milk. Fold in 1 tablespoon cocoa powder, 125 g (4 oz) plain flour, ½ teaspoon baking powder and 25 g (1 oz) each of white and milk chocolate chunks. Place dessertspoons of the mixture on to 2 baking sheets lined with nonstick baking paper, spacing them well apart. Flatten slightly and place in a preheated oven, 180°C (375°F), Gas Mark 4, for 5 minutes or until the edges are starting to firm. Remove from the oven and quickly sprinkle with 25 g (1 oz) mini marshmallows and 25 g (1 oz) each of white and dark chocolate chunks, pressing them down into the cookies. Return to the oven for a further 5–6 minutes until still slightly soft to the touch. Leave to cool on the baking sheet for 5 minutes, then transfer to a wire rack. Serve with scoops of vanilla ice cream. Store any leftover cookies in an airtight container.

 Rocky Road Clusters

Melt together 100 g (3½ oz) plain dark chocolate, broken into small pieces, 1 tablespoon golden syrup and 50 g (2 oz) unsalted butter in a small saucepan, stirring occasionally, until smooth and shiny. Stir in 125 g (4 oz) broken chocolate chip cookies and 75 g (3 oz) mini marshmallows. Spoon into 12 fairy cake cases and chill for 20 minutes until set. Serve with coffee. Store any leftover clusters in an airtight container for up to 3–4 days.

Sesame Banana Fritters with Peanut Butter Sauce

Serves 4

50 g (2 oz) self-raising flour
2 tablespoons sesame seeds
1 egg, separated
5 tablespoons cold milk
4 bananas, each cut into
    4 diagonal slices
vegetable oil, for frying

For the peanut butter sauce

150 g (5 oz) smooth
    peanut butter
grated rind and juice of 1 lime
100 ml (3½ fl oz) water

- To make the sauce, place the peanut butter, lime rind and juice and measurement water in a saucepan and cook over a low heat, stirring, until smooth.

- Place the flour and sesame seeds in a bowl and make a well in the centre. Add the egg yolk and milk and gradually whisk into the flour to form a thick batter. Whisk the egg white in a clean bowl with a hand-held electric whisk until stiff, then fold into the batter. Tip the bananas into the batter and stir lightly to coat.

- Heat about 5 cm (2 inches) of oil in a wok or large frying pan until a drop of batter rises to the surface surrounded by bubbles and starts to brown. Add the bananas and fry for 3–4 minutes until crisp. Remove with a slotted spoon and drain on kitchen paper.

- Serve immediately with the peanut butter sauce.

Pan-fried Banana, Peanut Butter and Choc Sandwiches Beat together 2 large eggs and 250 ml (8 fl oz) milk in a shallow dish. Spread 2 tablespoons peanut butter on 1 slice of white bread and chocolate spread on another slice. Thinly slice 1 large banana and place half on top of the peanut butter, then sandwich the bread slices together. Press down lightly. Place in the egg mixture and leave to soak, then turn over. Repeat to make 1 more sandwich. Heat a little unsalted butter in a large frying pan, add the sandwiches and cook for 2–3 minutes on each side until golden brown. Cut in half diagonally and serve one half per person.

Banana Bread and Peanut Butter Pudding Remove the crusts from 8 medium slices of white bread. Spread the slices with 100 g (3½ oz) smooth peanut butter, then cut each slice in half. Thinly slice 3 bananas and place half in the bottom of a buttered 1 litre (1¾ pint) ovenproof dish. Arrange the bread over the top and add the remaining bananas. Pour over a 500 g (1 lb) pot of fresh custard and leave to stand for 5 minutes. Sprinkle with 2 tablespoons demerara sugar, then place in a preheated oven, 180°C (350°F), Gas Mark 4, for 20 minutes, until bubbling.

30 Sticky Date, Maple Syrup and Pecan Puddings

Serves 6

150 g (5 oz) unsalted butter, diced, plus extra for greasing

175 g (6 oz) ready-to-eat pitted dates

200 ml (7 fl oz) cold water

50 ml (2 fl oz) maple syrup, plus 6 teaspoons

3 eggs, beaten

175 g (6 oz) self-raising flour

50 g (2 oz) pecan nuts, chopped

custard, to serve

- Lightly grease 6 x 150 ml (¼ pint) metal pudding moulds and place on a baking sheet. Place the dates and measurement water in a small saucepan and bring to the boil, then cover and simmer gently for 5–6 minutes. Transfer to a large bowl and mash them with the back of a spoon or fork.

- Stir in the butter and the 50 ml (2 fl oz) maple syrup and stir until the butter has melted, then gently stir in the eggs, flour and pecans.

- Place 1 teaspoonful of maple syrup in each of the prepared pudding moulds and spoon in the sponge mixture. Place in a preheated oven, 180°C (350°F), Gas Mark 4, for 20 minutes or until risen and firm to the touch. Leave to cool in the tins for a few minutes.

- Turn out the puddings into bowls and serve with custard.

---

1 Date and Maple Syrup Sauce

Place 50 g (2 oz) unsalted butter, 2 tablespoons soft light brown sugar, 2 tablespoons maple syrup and 100 g (3½ oz) chopped ready-to-eat pitted dates in a saucepan over a low heat and stir until the butter has melted and the sugar has dissolved. Stir in 3 tablespoons double cream and simmer for 2–3 minutes until thickened. Serve poured over ice cream.

2 Sticky Date and Maple Syrup Tart

Place a 20 cm (8 inch) shop-bought sweet pastry case on a baking sheet. Cut 15 Medjool dates in half and remove the stones. Place 75 g (3 oz) unsalted butter, 3 tablespoons maple syrup and 50 g (2 oz) soft light brown sugar in a saucepan and cook over a low heat, stirring, until the sugar has dissolved. Stir in 100 g (3½ oz) walnut or pecan pieces and the dates. Spoon the mixture into the pastry case. Place the tart in a preheated oven, 180°C (350°F), Gas Mark 4, for 12–15 minutes. Leave to cool slightly before serving.

30 Sherry Trifle

Serves 6–8

6 trifle sponges
100 ml (3½ fl oz) sweet sherry (optional)
150 g (5 oz) raspberry jam
1 tablespoon lemon juice
250 g (8 oz) raspberries
400 ml (14 fl oz) whipping cream
25 g (1 oz) toasted flaked almonds, to decorate

For the custard

500 ml (17 fl oz) milk
2 teaspoons vanilla extract
4 egg yolks
50 g (2 oz) caster sugar
2 teaspoons cornflour

- To make the custard, place the milk and vanilla extract in a saucepan and heat until just below boiling point. Place the egg yolks, sugar and cornflour in a heatproof bowl and beat with a hand-held electric whisk until pale and thick, then gradually whisk in the warm milk. Return to the pan and cook over a medium heat for 2–3 minutes, whisking continuously, until the custard has thickened. Transfer to a bowl, cover with clingfilm to prevent a skin forming and chill.

- Meanwhile, arrange the trifle sponges in the base of a 20 cm (8 inch) trifle bowl and pour over the sherry, if using. Mix together the jam and lemon juice in a bowl and spoon over the sponges. Add the raspberries and top with the cooled custard.

- Lightly whip the cream in a bowl with a hand-held electric whisk until it forms soft peaks. Spoon on top of the custard and decorate with the almonds. Serve immediately or chill until ready to serve.

 Quick Raspberry Trifles

Slice 350 g (11½ oz) shop-bought Madeira cake into 1 cm (½ inch) thick pieces and sandwich together with 100 g (3½ oz) raspberry jam. Cut into cubes, then divide between 6 glasses. Pour over 100 ml (3½ fl oz) sherry (optional) and top with 200 g (7 oz) raspberries. Spoon 500 g (1 lb) fresh vanilla custard over the top. Lightly whip 300 ml (½ pint) double cream in a bowl with a hand-held electric whisk until it forms soft peaks, then spoon over the top. Decorate with extra raspberries and serve immediately.

 Open Summer Trifle

Place 300 ml (½ pint) dessert wine (optional) and 6 tablespoons caster sugar in a saucepan and gently bring to the boil, then simmer for 7–8 minutes until syrupy. Cut 350 g (11½ oz) shop-bought Madeira or lemon sponge cake into thick pieces and divide between 6 plates, then drizzle over half the syrup. Lightly whip 400 ml (14 fl oz) double cream in a bowl with a hand-held electric whisk until it forms soft peaks, then spoon on top of the cakes. Top with 3 stoned and sliced peaches or nectarines and 175 g (6 oz) raspberries and drizzle with the remaining syrup. Serve immediately.

30 Key Lime Pie

Serves 6–8

225 g (7½ oz) digestive biscuits, crushed
100 g (3½ oz) unsalted butter, melted
3 large egg yolks
1 tablespoon grated lime rind
400 g (13 oz) can sweetened condensed milk
juice of 4–5 limes, about 150 ml (¼ pint)

To decorate

whipped cream
lime slices

- Stir the crushed biscuits into the melted butter and press into the base and sides of a 20 cm (8 inch) deep, loose-bottomed fluted flan tin. Place on a baking sheet and bake in a preheated oven, 180°C (350°F), Gas Mark 4, for 5 minutes.

- Meanwhile, place the egg yolks and lime rind in a bowl and beat with a hand-held electric whisk for 3–4 minutes until thickened. Pour in the condensed milk and continue whisking for a further 5 minutes. Whisk in the the lime juice.

- Pour the mixture into the tin and return to the oven for a further 8–10 minutes or until set. Leave to cool in the tin for 5 minutes, then chill for a further 5 minutes.

- Serve the pie in slices, decorated with whipped cream and lime slices.

 Chocolate, Lime and Mascarpone Creams Stir 150 g (5 oz) crushed plain chocolate digestive biscuits into 25 g (1 oz) melted unsalted butter and divide between 6 small glasses. Place 250 g (8 oz) mascarpone cheese, the rind and juice of 2 limes, 150 ml (¼ pint) double cream and 50 g (2 oz) icing sugar in a large bowl and whisk together with a hand-held electric whisk until thick. Spoon over the biscuits and top with a little grated chocolate. Serve immediately.

 No-bake Key Lime Pie Stir 225 g (7½ oz) crushed digestive biscuits into 75 g (3 oz) melted unsalted butter and press into the sides and base of a 20 cm (8 inch) deep, loose-bottomed fluted flan tin. Place 300 ml (½ pint) double cream, the juice and grated rind of 4 limes and 225 g (7½ oz) canned sweetened condensed milk in a large bowl and beat together with a hand-held electric whisk until thick and creamy. Spoon over the base and chill until ready to serve.

30 Creamy Lemon and Almond Rice Pudding

Serves 4

100 g (3½ oz) short-grain
  pudding rice, rinsed
50 g (2 oz) caster sugar
grated rind and juice of
  2 unwaxed lemons, plus extra
  rind to decorate
100 g (3½ oz) sultanas
450 ml (¾ pint) boiling water
410 g (13 oz) can evaporated milk
25 g (1 oz) flaked almonds

- Place the rice, sugar, lemon rind and juice, sultanas and measurement water in a saucepan and simmer, uncovered, for 20–25 minutes. Stir in the evaporated milk and simmer for a further 5 minutes until the rice is tender.

- Meanwhile, place the almonds in a hot frying pan and dry-fry for 1–2 minutes until toasted.

- Pour the rice pudding into warmed serving dishes and sprinkle with the flaked almonds and extra lemon rind. Serve immediately.

 Fast Lemon Rice Pudding Place 2 x 425 g (14 oz) cans creamed rice pudding in a saucepan and cook gently for 5–6 minutes until heated through. Stir in the grated rind and juice of 2 lemons and 100 g (3½ oz) sultanas. Serve sprinkled with 25 g (1 oz) toasted almonds.

 Fruity Cranberry and Sultana Risotto Place 150 g (5 oz) Arborio rice, 1 litre (1¾ pints) milk, 50 g (2 oz) sultanas, 25 g (1 oz) caster sugar, 50 g (2 oz) dried cranberries and 1 teaspoon vanilla extract in a large saucepan and bring to the boil. Reduce the heat and simmer, uncovered, for 15–20 minutes, stirring occasionally, until the rice is tender. Serve immediately.

 # Simple Sticky Toffee Puddings

Serves 4

50 g (2 oz) unsalted butter

150 g (5 oz) light muscovado sugar

25 ml (1 fl oz) golden syrup

1 teaspoon vanilla extract

150 ml (¼ pint) double cream

325 g (11 oz) shop-bought ginger cake, cut into 8 thick slices

vanilla ice cream, to serve (optional)

- Place the butter, sugar and golden syrup in a saucepan over a low heat and cook, stirring, until the sugar has dissolved. Bring to the boil, then gently bubble for 2–3 minutes. Add the vanilla extract and cream and stir well. Leave to cool slightly.

- Place 2 slices of the ginger cake in the bottom of 4 x 250 ml (8 fl oz) ovenproof dishes, then pour the toffee sauce over the top. Place on a baking sheet and bake in a preheated oven, 180°C (350°F), Gas Mark 4, for 12–15 minutes or until bubbling.

- Leave to stand for 4–5 minutes, then serve with scoops of vanilla ice cream, if using.

 Toffee and Ginger Sauce

Place 300 ml (½ pint) double cream and 125 g (4 oz) dark muscovado sugar in a saucepan and heat gently until the sugar has dissolved. Stir in 1 finely chopped piece of stem ginger in syrup and 2 tablespoons stem ginger syrup (taken from the jar) and bring to the boil, then cook for 2–3 minutes until thickened. Serve poured over ice cream.

 Cheat's Sticky Toffee Pudding

Thickly slice 325 g (11 oz) shop-bought ginger cake and place in a 900 ml (1½ pint) ovenproof dish. Pour over 250 ml (8 fl oz) shop-bought toffee sauce. Place in a preheated oven, 180°C (350°F), Gas Mark 4, for 15 minutes or until bubbling. Leave to stand for 2–3 minutes before serving with vanilla ice cream.

20 Mini Treacle Tarts

Serves 6–8

350 ml (12 fl oz) golden syrup
100 g (3½ oz) fresh white
 breadcrumbs
grated rind of 1 large lemon
1 egg, beaten
8 x 8 cm (3½ x 3½ inch) shop-
 bought sweet pastry cases
vanilla ice cream or double cream,
 to serve

- Place the golden syrup in a saucepan and heat gently until thinned in consistency. Remove from the heat and stir in the breadcrumbs, lemon rind and beaten egg. Transfer the mixture to a jug.

- Place the pastry cases on a baking sheet, then pour the filling evenly between them. Place in a preheated oven, 180°C (350°F), Gas Mark 4, for 12–15 minutes or until lightly set and golden.

- Leave to cool slightly, then serve warm with ice cream or double cream.

10 Treacly Banana Waffles

Place 125 ml (4 fl oz) golden syrup and 50 g (2 oz) chopped pecans in a small saucepan and heat gently until warmed through. Lightly toast 6 waffles and place in 6 bowls. Slice 6 bananas and arrange over the top of the waffles, then place a scoop of vanilla ice cream on each. Drizzle the warm pecan syrup over and serve immediately.

30 Treacle and Orange Tart

Place a 20 cm (8 inch) shop-bought sweet pastry case on a baking sheet. Place 300 ml (½ pint) golden syrup in a saucepan and heat gently until thinned in consistency. Remove from the heat and stir in 100 g (3½ oz) fresh white breadcrumbs, the grated rind of 1 orange and 1 beaten egg. Pour into the pastry case and bake in a preheated oven, 180°C (350°F), Gas Mark 4, for 15–20 minutes or until set. Serve warm.

DES-FAMI-VYV

30 Sticky Blueberry and Lemon Sponge Puddings

Serves 4

100 g (3½ oz) unsalted butter,
softened, plus extra
for greasing
1 lemon
4 teaspoons golden syrup
100 g (3½ oz) caster sugar
2 large eggs
100 g (3½ oz) self-raising flour,
sifted
125 g (4 oz) blueberries
custard or single cream, to serve
(optional)

- Lightly grease 4 x 200 ml (7 fl oz) metal pudding moulds and line the bases with nonstick baking paper. Place on a baking sheet. Grate the rind from the lemon, cut in half and then cut 4 thin slices from 1 half, reserving the remaining half.

- Place a lemon slice in the bottom of each prepared pudding mould, then drizzle 1 teaspoon of the golden syrup over each.

- Place the butter, sugar and grated lemon rind in a large bowl and beat with a hand-held electric whisk until light and fluffy. Whisk in the eggs, then squeeze over the juice of the remaining lemon half. Fold in the flour and blueberries.

- Spoon the mixture into the pudding moulds and spread the tops level. Place in a preheated oven, 190°C (375°F), Gas Mark 5, for 15–20 minutes or until risen and firm to the touch. Leave to cool in the tins for a few minutes. Turn out the puddings on to plates and serve with cream or custard, if using.

 Blueberry Sponges with Lemon Cream Roughly chop 2 blueberry muffins and divide between 4 bowls. Place 250 g (8 oz) blueberries, 50 g (2 oz) caster sugar and 2 tablespoons lemon juice in a saucepan and cook over a low heat, stirring, until the sugar has dissolved and the berries start to burst, then spoon the berries and juice over the sponges. Place 200 ml (7 fl oz) crème fraîche, 200 g (7 oz) Greek yogurt, 1 tablespoon icing sugar, 2 teaspoons grated lemon rind and 1 tablespoon lemon juice in a bowl and beat together. Spoon over the blueberries and serve immediately.

 Lemon and Blueberry Mess Place 125 g (4 oz) blueberries, 1 tablespoon caster sugar and the juice of 1 lemon in a saucepan and bring to the boil. Reduce the heat and simmer for 5 minutes until the berries start to break down. Press through a sieve into a bowl to make a coulis, then leave to cool. Whip 150 ml (¼ pint) double cream in a bowl with a hand-held electric whisk until just beginning to thicken, then fold in 300 g (10 oz) Greek yogurt, 3 tablespoons lemon curd, 2 crushed meringue nests and 100 g (3½ oz) blueberries. Spoon a third of the cream mixture into a large serving dish. Drizzle with a tablespoon of the coulis. Repeat this twice, then finish with a layer of the cream and a drizzle of coulis. Serve immediately.

30 Apple Tart

Serves 6–8

375 g (12 oz) pack chilled
   all-butter puff pastry
flour, for dusting
5 dessert apples, cored and cut
   into thin slices
juice of 1 lemon
50 g (2 oz) unsalted butter, diced
3 tablespoons caster sugar
4 tablespoons apricot jam
vanilla ice cream, to serve
   (optional)

- Line a large baking sheet with nonstick baking paper. Roll out the pastry on to a lightly floured surface to a 35 cm (14 inch) square, trimming the edges if necessary, to make a neat square. Place on the baking sheet and scrunch up the edges of the pastry to prevent the filling running out.

- Toss the apples in the lemon juice. Dot some of the butter over the base of the pastry and sprinkle with 1 tablespoon of the sugar.

- Arrange the apples in neat rows on the pastry, then dot with the remaining butter and sprinkle over the remaining sugar.

- Place in a preheated oven, 220°C (425°F), Gas Mark 7, for 15–20 minutes or until golden and crisp.

- Warm the apricot jam in a small saucepan, then brush over the apples and pastry. Serve immediately with scoops of vanilla ice cream, if using.

 Speedy Apple Compote

Melt 50 g (2 oz) unsalted butter in a saucepan, then add 4 peeled, cored and chopped apples, 2 tablespoons caster sugar and ½ teaspoon ground cinnamon. Cook for 4–5 minutes, stirring occasionally, until the apples have softened. Serve with dollops of vanilla yogurt.

 Individual Apple Tarts

Unroll a 375 g (12 oz) pack chilled ready-rolled puff pastry and cut out 6 x 16 x 8 cm (6½ x 3½ inch) rectangles, then place on a baking sheet. Using a sharp knife, score a 1 cm (½ inch) border around the edge, but do not cut all the way through. Prick the centre of each base with a fork. Divide half of 25 g (1 oz) diced unsalted butter over the bases and sprinkle with 1 tablespoon caster sugar. Arrange 4 cored and sliced apples between the bases and dot with the remaining butter and scatter over another tablespoon of caster sugar. Bake in a preheated oven, 200°C (400°F), Gas Mark 6, for 12–15 minutes or until risen and golden. Brush 2 tablespoons warmed apricot jam over the top of each and serve immediately.

3⬤ Baked New York Cheesecakes

Serves 6

75 g (3 oz) digestive biscuits, crushed

25 g (1 oz) unsalted butter, melted

200 g (7 oz) light cream cheese

50 g (2 oz) caster sugar

50 g (2 oz) soured cream

finely grated rind of ½ lemon

1 teaspoon vanilla extract

1 tablespoon cornflour

2 eggs

raspberries, to serve

icing sugar, for dusting

- Line a 6-hole muffin tin with paper cases. Stir the crushed biscuits into the melted butter and press into the bases of the cases. Chill while you make the filling.

- Place the cream cheese, sugar, soured cream, lemon rind, vanilla extract, cornflour and eggs in a bowl and beat together.

- Spoon the mixture over the biscuit bases and place in a preheated oven, 160°C (325°F), Gas Mark 3, for 20 minutes. Leave to cool in the tin for 5 minutes.

- Remove the cheesecakes from the cases and place on a serving plate. Serve warm decorated with raspberries and a dusting of icing sugar.

 Instant New York Cheesecakes

Place 200 g (7 oz) cream cheese, 2 tablespoons icing sugar, 125 g (4 oz) soured cream, ½ teaspoon vanilla extract and 1 tablespoon grated lemon rind in a bowl and beat together. Spoon the mixture on to 12 digestive biscuits and decorate each with 2 raspberries. Serve 2 biscuits per person.

 New York Cheesecake

in a Glass Crush 7 digestive biscuits and divide between 6 glasses. Place 350 g (11½ oz) cream cheese, 200 g (7 oz) soured cream, 2 tablespoons icing sugar, 1 teaspoon vanilla extract and the grated rind of ½ lemon in a bowl and beat together. Spoon into the glasses, top with a few raspberries and chill for 10 minutes before serving.

30 Chocolate and Apricot Crunch

Serves 4

200 g (7 oz) orange-flavoured
 plain dark chocolate
 (70% cocoa solids)
125 g (4 oz) unsalted butter
1 tablespoon golden syrup
4 meringue nests, broken into
 small pieces
125 g (4 oz) chocolate chip
 cookies, broken into pieces
150 g (5 oz) ready-to-eat dried
 apricots, chopped
cocoa powder, for dusting

- Line an 18 x 28 cm (7 x 11 inch) rectangular cake tin with nonstick baking paper. Place the chocolate, butter and golden syrup in a small saucepan and heat gently, stirring occasionally, until smooth and shiny.

- Place all remaining ingredients in a large bowl and mix well, then pour over the chocolate mixture. Stir until all the ingredients are evenly coated.

- Tip the mixture into the prepared tin and even out the mixture with the back of a spoon. Place in the freezer for 10 minutes, then chill in the refrigerator for a further 10 minutes until firm.

- Run a knife around the edge of the tin, turn out on to a board and remove the baking paper. Dust the surface with cocoa powder and cut into 16 slices. Store any leftover bars in an airtight container for up to 3–4 days.

 Chocolate and Apricot Crunch Layer Mix together 500 g (1 lb) Greek yogurt and 25 g (1 oz) sifted icing sugar in a bowl. Spoon half the mixture into 4 glasses, then top each with 2 canned apricot halves. Divide 50 g (2 oz) chocolate granola between the glasses, then spoon the remaining yogurt over the top. Serve immediately.

 Nutty Chocolate Crunch Place 100 g (3½ oz) milk chocolate, 2 tablespoons golden syrup and 25 g (1 oz) unsalted butter in a saucepan and heat gently, stirring, until melted, then stir in 125 g (4 oz) granola with nuts. Tip the mixture on to a baking sheet lined with nonstick baking paper and chill for 10–15 minutes. To serve, roughly break up the granola and spoon over ice cream.

30 Lemon Meringue Pie

Serves 6

20 cm (8 inch) shop-bought
    sweet pastry case
405 g (13 oz) can light
    condensed milk
2 eggs yolks
grated rind and juice of 2 lemons

For the meringue

4 egg whites
200 g (7 oz) caster sugar

- Place the pastry case on a baking sheet. Place the condensed milk, egg yolks and lemon rind and juice in a large bowl and beat together. Pour into the pastry case to 1 cm (½ inch) below the top.

- Whisk the egg whites in a clean large bowl with a hand-held electric whisk until they form soft peaks, then gradually whisk in the sugar until the mixture is thick and glossy.

- Pile the meringue on top of the lemon mixture and place in a preheated oven, 190°C (375°F), Gas Mark 5, for 15–20 minutes until golden and crisp.

 1 **Lemon Meringue Kisses**

Lightly whip 300 ml (½ pint) double cream in a bowl with a hand-held electric whisk until it forms soft peaks, then stir in 2–3 tablespoons lemon curd. Sandwich together 24 mini meringue shells with the lemon cream. Serve 2 meringues per person, dusted with icing sugar.

 2 **Meringue and Lemon Curd Mess**

Roughly crush 8 meringue nests into different sizes. Lightly whip 300 ml (½ pint) double cream in a large bowl with a hand-held electric whisk until it forms soft peaks, then stir in 2–3 tablespoons lemon curd to taste and 150 g (5 oz) Greek yogurt. Gently stir in the crushed meringues, then spoon into 6 glasses. Drizzle the tops with a little extra lemon curd. Chill for 10 minutes before serving.

3 ◑ Mincemeat and Apple Strudel

Serves 6

2 small dessert apples, peeled,
   cored and diced
250 g (8 oz) mincemeat
50 g (2 oz) pecan nuts, chopped
4 sheets of filo pastry, about
   48 x 25 cm (19 x 10 inches)
50 g (2 oz) unsalted butter,
   melted
icing sugar, for dusting
vanilla ice cream, to serve
   (optional)

- Mix together the apples, mincemeat and pecan nuts in a bowl.

- Lay the first sheet of filo pastry on a clean tea towel on the work surface and brush with melted butter. Repeat with the remaining sheets of pastry.

- Spread the mincemeat mixture over the pastry, leaving a 2.5 cm (1 inch) border. Fold in the ends over the filling, then roll up like a Swiss roll, from one long edge, using the tea towel. Once rolled up, press the strudel gently together. Place on a baking sheet and brush with the remaining butter.

- Place in a preheated oven, 180°C (350°F), Gas Mark 4, for about 20 minutes or until golden brown. Dust with icing sugar and serve with scoops of vanilla ice cream, if using.

1 ◑ Mincemeat Purses

Fold 12 x 48 x 25 cm (19 x 10 inch) sheets of filo pastry in half and brush with melted unsalted butter. Place 25 g (1 oz) mincemeat in the centre of each square, then draw up the edges and scrunch together. Place on a baking sheet and brush with melted butter. Place in a preheated oven, 190°C (375°F), Gas Mark 5, for 6–8 minutes or until golden. Serve 2 parcels per person, dusted with icing sugar.

2 ◑ Mini Mincemeat and Apple Pies

Unroll a 375 g (12 oz) pack chilled ready-rolled puff pastry and cut out 12 x 10 cm (4 inch) circles. Place the circles on a baking sheet. Using a 8 cm (3½ inch) cutter, press into the centre of each disc to make an indent, but do not cut all the way through. Brush the edge of each disc with a little milk. Mix together 375 g (12 oz) mincemeat, 1 peeled, cored and diced dessert apple and 25 g (1 oz) dried cranberries in a bowl. Spoon about a dessertspoon of mincemeat mixture into the centre of each disc, then sprinkle over 50 g (2 oz) chopped pecans. Place on the top shelf of a preheated oven, 220°C (425°F), Gas Mark 7, for 12–15 minutes or until golden. Serve 2 warm pies per person, dusted with icing sugar.

Caramel Dipping Sauce with Fresh Fruit

Serves 4–6

75 g (3 oz) unsalted butter
175 g (6 oz) soft light
   brown sugar
2 tablespoons golden syrup
1 teaspoon vanilla extract
150 ml (¼ pint) double cream
apple wedges and bananas
   chunks, for dipping

- Place the butter, sugar, golden syrup and vanilla extract in a heavy-based nonstick saucepan and stir over a low heat until the butter has melted and the sugar has dissolved. Add the cream, stirring continuously. Bring back to the boil and simmer for 5 minutes until thickened.

- Pour into a bowl and leave to stand for a few minutes before serving with the apples and bananas, for dipping.

 Hazelnut and Caramel Sauce

Place 50 g (2 oz) chopped hazelnuts in a frying pan and dry-fry over a medium heat for 2–3 minutes, stirring occasionally, until toasted. Place 75 g (3 oz) caster sugar and 90 ml (3¼ fl oz) water in a small heavy-based saucepan and heat gently until the sugar has dissolved. Bring to the boil and boil rapidly until the caramel is a deep golden colour. Immerse the base of the pan in cold water to prevent the caramel becoming too dark. Carefully add 2 tablespoons water, then stir in the hazelnuts and 50 g (2 oz) unsalted butter until the sauce is smooth and glossy. Serve poured over ice cream.

 Hazelnut Caramel Brittle

Line a baking sheet with a lightly oiled piece of foil. Melt 100 g (3½ oz) caster sugar in a heavy-based saucepan over a low heat. Do not stir the sugar, but gently shake the pan from time to time to redistribute the sugar and prevent it from overcooking in one place. When all the sugar has melted and turned a rich golden caramel colour, quickly stir in 100 g (3½ oz) roughly chopped toasted hazelnuts. Pour out immediately on to the oiled foil and leave to cool and harden. When set, place in a strong food bag and bash with a rolling pin. Serve sprinkled over ice cream or chocolate mousse.

Quick Rosewater and Cardamom Rice Pudding

Serves 4–6

2 x 425 g (14 oz) cans rice pudding
2 teaspoons rosewater
6 cardamom pods, crushed
50 g (2 oz) pistachio nuts, chopped

- Place the rice pudding in a saucepan, stir in the rosewater and cardamom pods and cook gently for 5–6 minutes until heated through. Stir in 25 g (1 oz) of the pistachios.

- Serve in bowls decorated with the remaining pistachios.

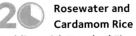 **Rosewater and Cardamom Rice Pudding with Poached Figs**

Place 125 g (4 oz) sugar, 300 ml (½ pint) water and 2 teaspoons rosewater in a saucepan and stir over a medium heat until the sugar has dissolved, then bring to the boil and cook for 5 minutes. Reduce the heat and add 8 halved figs. Cook gently for 8–10 minutes until tender. Meanwhile, make the rice pudding as above. Serve with the poached figs and their syrup and sprinkled with the pistachios.

 Homemade Spiced Rice Pudding

Place 100 g (3½ oz) rinsed pudding rice, 50 g (2 oz) caster sugar, 2 teaspoons rosewater, 6 crushed cardamom pods and 450 ml (¾ pint) boiling water in a saucepan and simmer, uncovered, for 20–25 minutes. Stir in a 410 g (13 oz) can evaporated milk and simmer for a further 5 minutes. Spoon into 4 bowls and serve decorated with chopped pistachios.

Chocolate Fondue with Hazelnut Straws

Serves 6

200 g (7 oz) plain dark chocolate (75% cocoa solids), broken into pieces
300 ml (½ pint) double cream
25 g (1 oz) unsalted butter
2 tablespoons brandy or orange liqueur (optional)

For the filo straws

3 sheets of filo pastry, about 25 x 23 cm (10 x 9 inches)
25 g (1 oz) unsalted butter, melted
25 g (1 oz) caster sugar
50 g (2 oz) chopped hazelnuts

- To make the filo straws, line a baking sheet with nonstick baking paper. Place 1 sheet of filo pastry on the baking sheet, brush with a third of the melted butter and sprinkle over a third of the sugar and hazelnuts. Continue with the remaining ingredients, finishing with the hazelnuts and sugar on top.

- Cut the pastry in half lengthways, then cut into 28 strips, about 1 cm (½ inch) wide and separate slightly. Place in a preheated oven, 180°C (350°F), Gas Mark 4, for 4–5 minutes or until golden. Leave to cool on a wire rack while you make the fondue.

- Place the chocolate, cream, butter and brandy or orange liqueur, if using, in a heatproof bowl set over a saucepan of gently simmering water. Heat gently for 5–7 minutes, stirring occasionally, until the mixture is smooth and glossy.

- Pour into a fondue pot or warm bowl and serve immediately with the hazelnut straws, for dipping.

10 **Hazelnut Straws with Ice cream and Chocolate Sauce** Make the hazelnut straws as above. Meanwhile, place 300 ml (½ pint) shop-bought Belgian chocolate sauce and 1 tablespoon orange liqueur (optional) in a small saucepan and heat gently to warm through. Dip 6 x 100 g (3½ oz) individual tubs of vanilla ice cream in hot water and turn out. Drizzle with the chocolate sauce and serve with the warm hazelnut straws.

30 **Chocolate Fondue with Puff Pastry Hazelnut Straws** Whizz 75 g (3 oz) hazelnuts in a food processor until finely chopped, then add 1 teaspoon ground cinnamon and 1 tablespoon caster sugar and pulse together. Sprinkle some of the mixture on a clean work surface and unroll a 375 g (12 oz) pack chilled ready-rolled puff pastry on top. Sprinkle over half the nut mixture, press into the pastry, then roll out to a 30 x 23 cm (12 x 9 inch) rectangle. Sprinkle over the remaining nut mixture and gently roll it in. Cut widthways into 1 cm (½ inch) wide strips and then twist them. Place on a large baking sheet and bake in a preheated oven, 200°C (400°F), Gas Mark 6, for 15–20 minutes or until golden. Meanwhile, make the fondue as above and serve with the warm straws.

QuickCook
Entertaining

Recipes listed by cooking time

30

20

10

2 Tiramisu

Serves 4–6

250 g (8 oz) mascarpone cheese
250 g (8 oz) shop-bought fresh
  vanilla custard
3 tablespoons Marsala or brandy
150 ml (¼ pint) cold strong
  black coffee
16–18 sponge fingers
2 tablespoons cocoa powder

- Place the mascarpone, custard, Marsala or brandy and 1 tablespoon of the coffee in a large bowl and beat with a hand-held electric whisk for 2–3 minutes until light, fluffy and smooth.

- Take one sponge finger at a time and dip into the cold coffee, taking care not to let the sponge get too soggy. Line a shallow dish with half the sponge fingers or divide between shallow individual dishes. Spoon over half the creamy mixture, then sift over half the cocoa powder.

- Repeat with the remaining coffee-dipped sponge fingers, cream and cocoa powder. Chill until ready to serve.

1 Tiramisu Affogato

Place 200 ml (7 fl oz) whipping cream, 1 tablespoon icing sugar and 1 tablespoon Marsala (optional) in a bowl and whisk with a hand-held electric whisk until it forms soft peaks. Place 1 scoop of vanilla ice cream and 1 scoop of coffee ice cream in each of 4 heatproof glasses or cups. Top each with 1 Italian Savoiardi (ladyfinger) biscuit. Pour a shot of hot espresso over each and spoon on the lightly whipped cream. Dust with a little cocoa powder and serve immediately.

3 Strawberry and White Chocolate

Tiramisu Melt 150 g (5 oz) white chocolate, broken into small pieces, in a heatproof bowl set over a saucepan of gently simmering water. Place 250 g (8 oz) mascarpone cheese and 250 g (8 oz) shop-bought fresh vanilla custard in a bowl and beat in the melted chocolate. Dip 16 sponge fingers in 200 ml (7 fl oz) sweet dessert wine and place half in the bottom of a shallow dish. Cover with 350 g (11½ oz) hulled and sliced strawberries, reserving a few for decoration, then spoon over half the chocolate mixture. Repeat the sponge and chocolate layers. Chill for 10 minutes, then serve decorated with the reserved strawberries.

1⏱ Affogato al Caffe

Serves 4

8 balls of good-quality vanilla
   ice cream
4 freshly made espresso coffees
8 amaretti biscuits, to serve

- Scoop 2 balls of the ice cream into each of 4 cappuccino cups or latte glasses. Pour a cup of hot coffee quickly over each.

- Serve immediately, with the biscuits for dunking.

 Affogato al Caffe with Vanilla Syrup

Place 225 g (7½ oz) caster sugar, 250 ml (8 fl oz) water and 1 vanilla pod, split lengthways and seeds scraped out, in a saucepan. Stir over a low heat until the sugar has dissolved, then increase the heat and simmer for 6 minutes. Scoop the ice cream into 4 heatproof cups or glasses as above. Remove the vanilla pod from the pan and spoon 1 tablespoon of the syrup over each ice cream, before pouring over the hot coffee as above. The remaining syrup can be poured over fruit.

 Affogato al Caffe with Almond

Macaroons Mix together 50 g (2 oz) ground almonds and 75 g (3 oz) caster sugar in a bowl. Whisk 1 large egg white and ¼ teaspoon almond extract in a clean bowl with a hand-held electric whisk until stiff, then fold in the ground almond mixture. Place teaspoons of the mixture, slightly apart, on 2 large baking sheets lined with nonstick baking paper. Place in preheated oven, 180°C (350°F), Gas Mark 4, for 15 minutes. Cool on the baking sheets for 5 minutes, then place on a wire rack. Make the above recipe and serve with the macaroons for dunking.

30 Lemon and Lime Self-saucing Puddings

Serves 4

50 g (2 oz) unsalted butter, softened
125 g (4 oz) caster sugar
grated rind and juice of 1 small lemon
grated rind and juice of 1 lime
2 large eggs, separated
50 g (2 oz) self-raising flour
300 ml (½ pint) milk

- Place the butter, sugar and lemon and lime rind in a large bowl and beat with a hand-held electric whisk until light and fluffy. Add the egg yolks and flour and beat in (the mixture will look curdled), then whisk in the lemon and lime juice and milk.

- Whisk the egg whites in a clean bowl with a hand-held electric whisk until stiff, then gently fold into the lemon and lime mixture.

- Put 4 x 200 ml (7 fl oz) ovenproof dishes in a roasting tin and pour the pudding mixture into the dishes. Pour enough water into the tin to come halfway up the sides of the dishes.

- Place in a preheated oven, 180°C (350°F), Gas Mark 4, for 20 minutes or until the tops are golden brown and spongy and there is a lovely lemon and lime sauce in the bottom. Serve immediately.

 Lime Curd Tarts
Melt 75 g (3 oz) unsalted butter in a heavy-based saucepan, then add 3 large eggs, 75 g (3 oz) caster sugar, 125 ml (4 fl oz) lime juice and the grated rind of 1 lime. Cook over a low heat, whisking continuously, until it has thickened and formed a custard. Spoon into 4 x 8 cm (3½ inch) shop-bought sweet pastry cases and serve warm.

Lemon and Lime Syllabubs
Place 50 g (2 oz) caster sugar, the juice of ½ lemon and 1 lime and 1 teaspoon each finely grated lemon and lime rind in a bowl and stir to dissolve the sugar. Lightly whip 200 ml (7 fl oz) double cream in a bowl with a hand-held electric whisk until it forms soft peaks, then slowly whisk in 100 ml (3½ fl oz) sweet white wine. Whisk in the sugar mixture until the cream is thick and fluffy. Spoon into 4 glasses and decorate with a little lemon and lime rind. Serve immediately or chill until ready to serve.

Tangy Lemon Tarts

Serves 8

8 x 8 cm (3½ inch) shop-bought
  sweet pastry cases
50 g (2 oz) granulated sugar
100 ml (3½ fl oz) water
1 unwaxed lemon, cut into
  8 thin slices

For the lemon filling

2 large eggs
75 g (3 oz) caster sugar
finely grated rind and juice of
  2 unwaxed lemons
100 ml (3½ fl oz) double cream

- To make the lemon filling, place all the ingredients in a food processor or blender and blend until smooth. Transfer to a jug.

- Place the pastry cases on a baking sheet and pour in the lemon filling. Place in the centre of a preheated oven, 150°C (300°F), Gas Mark 2, for about 15 minutes or until just set. Leave to cool slightly.

- Meanwhile, place the granulated sugar and measurement water in a saucepan and heat gently, stirring occasionally, until the sugar has completely dissolved. Add the lemon slices and simmer, uncovered, for 12–15 minutes. Tip on to a piece of nonstick baking paper to cool slightly.

- Serve the warm tarts topped with the lemon slices.

 Instant Lemon Tarts

Place 250 g (8 oz) mascarpone cheese and 6–8 tablespoons lemon curd, to taste, in a bowl and whisk together. Spoon into 8 x 8 cm (3½ inch) shop-bought sweet pastry cases and serve, dusted with icing sugar.

 No-cook Lemon Tart

Stir 225 g (7½ oz) crushed digestive biscuits into 75 g (3 oz) melted unsalted butter and press into the sides and base of a 20 cm (8 inch) deep, loose-bottomed fluted flan tin. Chill while you make the filling. Place 300 ml (½ pint) double cream, the juice and grated rind of 2 lemons, 225 g (7½ oz) canned sweetened condensed milk and 2 tablespoons lemon curd in a large bowl and whisk together with a hand-held electric whisk until thick and creamy. Spoon over the base. Chill for 10 minutes before serving.

White Chocolate and Raspberry Meringue Roulade

Serves 6

150 g (5 oz) raspberries
25 g (1 oz) white chocolate, melted, to serve

For the meringue

5 egg whites
225 g (7½ oz) caster sugar
½ teaspoon white wine vinegar
1 teaspoon cornflour
½ teaspoon vanilla extract

For the chocolate filling

150 g (5 oz) white chocolate, broken into small pieces
150 ml (¼ pint) crème fraîche

- To make the chocolate filling, melt the chocolate in a heatproof bowl set over a saucepan of gently simmering water, then leave to cool slightly. Place the crème fraîche in a bowl and stir in the melted chocolate. Chill while you make the meringue.

- Line a 20 x 30 cm (8 x 12 inch) Swiss roll tin with nonstick baking paper. Whisk the egg whites in a clean large bowl with a hand-held electric whisk until stiff, then gradually whisk in the sugar until the mixture is thick and glossy. Gently fold in the vinegar, cornflour and vanilla extract.

- Spread the mixture into the prepared tin and place in the centre of a preheated oven, 180°C (350°F), Gas Mark 4, for 15 minutes. Leave to cool in the tin for 5 minutes.

- Turn out the meringue on to another piece of baking paper and spread the chocolate filling evenly over the top. Sprinkle with the raspberries and roll up the meringue.

- Transfer to a serving plate and drizzle with the melted white chocolate before serving.

 Raspberry and White Chocolate Mini Pavlovas Melt 150 g (5 oz) white chocolate, broken into small pieces, in a heatproof bowl set over a saucepan of gently simmering water, then leave to cool slightly. Place 150 ml (¼ pint) crème fraîche in a bowl and stir in the melted chocolate. Fill 6 meringue nests with the chocolate mixture, then top with 150 g (5 oz) raspberries. Decorate with a little grated white chocolate. Serve immediately or chill until ready to serve.

 White Chocolate and Raspberry Meringue Creams Melt 175 g (6 oz) white chocolate, broken into small pieces, in a heatproof bowl set over a saucepan of gently simmering water. Cool slightly, then stir in 300 ml (½ pint) crème fraîche. Roughly break up 6 meringue nests and divide between 6 glasses. Divide 200 g (7 oz) raspberries between the glasses, reserving a few for decoration, then spoon over the chocolate mixture. Top with the reserved raspberries and a little grated white chocolate. Chill until ready to serve.

Salted Caramel Shards

Serves 4

100 g (3½ oz) caster sugar
1 teaspoon coarse sea salt
chocolate ice cream, to serve

- Line a baking sheet with nonstick baking paper. Place the sugar in a small heavy-based saucepan over a low heat. Do not stir. Watch the sugar until the bottom layer has melted, then reduce the heat and stir until the sugar has dissolved and is a light caramel colour.

- Pour on to the baking sheet, sprinkle with the sea salt and leave to harden.

- When set, after about 10 minutes, use a rolling pin to break into shards.

- Serve with chocolate ice cream or as a decoration for fools or syllabubs.

 Salted Caramel Sauce

Place 100 g (3½ oz) unsalted butter, 75 g (3 oz) soft light brown sugar, 75 ml (3 fl oz) golden syrup, 1 teaspoon vanilla extract and 1 teaspoon coarse sea salt in a saucepan and melt over a medium heat. Pour in 300 ml (½ pint) double cream and boil for 5 minutes until thickened slightly. Serve poured over ice cream.

 Chocolate Salted Caramel Medallions

Make the caramel shards as above. Melt 100 g (3½ oz) plain dark chocolate, broken into small pieces, in a heatproof bowl set over a saucepan of gently simmering water. Meanwhile, draw circles about 4 cm (1¾ inches) in diameter on to a large sheet of nonstick baking paper, turn the paper over and use the lines as a guide. Spoon about ½ teaspoon of the melted chocolate inside each circle. Sprinkle over some salted caramel shards and leave to set. Serve as an accompaniment to ice cream.

 Irish Coffee Syllabubs

Serves 4

100 g (3½ oz) caster sugar
4 tablespoons cold strong
   black coffee
4 tablespoons coffee liqueur
300 ml (½ pint) double cream
cocoa powder, for dusting

For the topping

150 ml (¼ pint) whipping cream
2 teaspoons vanilla sugar
2 tablespoons Irish whiskey
   (optional)
4 tablespoons ice-cold water

- Place the caster sugar, coffee, liqueur and double cream in a large bowl and beat with a hand-held electric whisk until thickened and the whisk leaves a trail when lifted above the mixture. Pour into 4 tall glasses and chill while you make the topping.

- To make the topping, place the whipping cream, vanilla sugar, whiskey, if using, and measurement water in a bowl and beat with a hand-held electric whisk until thick and frothy.

- Spoon the cappuccino topping over the syllabubs and dust with cocoa powder. Serve immediately or chill until ready to serve.

Irish Coffee Ice Creams

Place 2 scoops of vanilla ice cream in 4 heatproof glasses or cups, then add a shot of Irish whiskey to each. Pour 200 ml (7 fl oz) freshly made strong black coffee over each and serve immediately.

Irish Coffee Creams

Dissolve 2 teaspoons espresso coffee powder in 2 tablespoons boiling water. Place 200 g (7 oz) mascarpone cheese and 2 tablespoons icing sugar in a heatproof bowl and whisk in the coffee mixture with a hand-held electric whisk until smooth. Whisk in 200 ml (7 fl oz) double cream and 2 tablespoons Irish whiskey and beat until creamy. Spoon into 4 glasses and chill for 10 minutes before serving.

1 Pan-fried Figs with Marsala

Serves 4

50 g (2 oz) unsalted butter
8 large ripe figs, halved
2 tablespoons light muscovado sugar
75 ml (3 fl oz) Marsala
crème fraîche or mascarpone cheese, to serve

- Melt the butter in a nonstick frying pan and place the figs into the frothing butter, cut side down. Fry for about 2 minutes until golden, then turn over.

- Sprinkle the sugar over the figs and cook for 2 minutes. Pour in the Marsala and allow it to bubble up, then reduce the heat and simmer for a further 2–3 minutes to reduce the alcohol and produce a syrupy sauce.

- Spoon into bowls and serve immediately with dollops of crème fraîche or mascarpone cheese.

---

2 Figs with Marsala Sabayon

Grease 4 x 200 ml (7 fl oz) ovenproof dishes or ramekins and place on a baking sheet. Stand 2 halves of a large fig in each. Place 5 egg yolks, 2 tablespoons caster sugar, 2 tablespoons honey and 75 ml (3 fl oz) Marsala in a heatproof bowl set over a pan of simmering water and whisk with a hand-held electric whisk for about 8 minutes until the mixture is thick and the whisk leaves a trail when lifted above the mixture. Remove from the heat and continue to whisk for a further 4 minutes until cooled. Spoon the mixture over the figs and cook under a preheated hot grill for 2–3 minutes or until golden. Serve immediately.

3 Roasted Figs with Honey and Marsala

Cut a deep cross into 8 figs and place in an ovenproof dish that has a lid. Drizzle over 2 tablespoons honey and 4 tablespoons Marsala. Cover with the lid and place in a preheated oven, 200°C (400°F), Gas Mark 6, for about 20 minutes. Serve with the juices and dollops of mascarpone cheese.

 # Vanilla Poached Pears with Warm Fudge Sauce

Serves 4

50 g (2 oz) caster sugar
1 vanilla pod, split lengthways
  and seeds scraped out
1 tablespoon lemon juice
600 ml (1 pint) cold water
4 ripe dessert pears, peeled,
  halved and cored
vanilla ice cream, to serve
  (optional)

For the fudge sauce

75 g (3 oz) unsalted butter
150 g (5 oz) soft light
  brown sugar
170 g (6 oz) can evaporated milk
1 tablespoon golden syrup

- Place the caster sugar, vanilla pod and seeds, lemon juice and measurement water in a large pan and bring gradually to the boil, stirring occasionally, until the sugar has dissolved. Add the pears and simmer gently for 10–15 minutes or until tender.

- Meanwhile, place all the fudge sauce ingredients in a saucepan and cook gently over a low heat for 2–3 minutes or until the butter has melted. Gently bring to the boil, stirring continuously, for 3–4 minutes until the sauce has thickened slightly. Remove from the heat and keep warm.

- Drain the pears from the syrup, divide between 4 serving plates and pour the fudge sauce over the top. Serve immediately with vanilla ice cream, if using.

 Pear and Fudge Sauce Ice Cream Sundaes Make the fudge sauce as above. Peel, core and chop 4 ripe pears and divide between 4 sundae glasses. Add 1 large scoop of vanilla ice cream to each glass, then crumble 1 florentine biscuit over each sundae. Top with the warm fudge sauce and serve immediately.

 Baked Fudgy Pears with Florentines Peel and cut 4 pears in half lengthways. Scoop out the core with a teaspoon to make a hole. Place in an ovenproof dish and drizzle over the juice of 1 lemon. Mix together 50 g (2 oz) soft light brown sugar and 50 g (2 oz) softened unsalted butter in a bowl and dot over the pears. Place in a preheated oven, 180°C (350°F), Gas Mark 4, for 10 minutes. Remove from the oven and add a crumbled chocolate florentine into each hole, then pour over 170 g (6 oz) can evaporated milk and stir. Return to the oven for a further 10 minutes, stirring the sauce once. Transfer the pears to 4 serving plates and pour over the sauce.

3 Raspberry Millefeuille

Serves 6

375 g (12 oz) pack chilled
   ready-rolled puff pastry
300 ml (½ pint) double cream
2 tablespoons raspberry liqueur
   (optional)
250 g (8 oz) raspberries
icing sugar, for dusting

· Line a large baking sheet with nonstick baking paper. Unroll the pastry and place on the baking sheet. Prick all over with a fork and cover with another piece of baking paper. Place a wire rack on top (this prevents the pastry rising too much).

· Place in a preheated oven, 220°C (425°F), Gas Mark 7, for 10 minutes. Using an oven glove, carefully remove the wire rack and baking paper and turn over the pastry. Return to the oven for a further 5 minutes or until browned. Cool on a wire rack.

· Meanwhile, lightly whip the cream and liqueur, if using, in a bowl with a hand-held electric whisk until it forms soft peaks.

· Cut the pastry into 3 even-sized strips. Place 1 strip of pastry on a large serving plate and spoon over half the cream and half the raspberries. Repeat the layers, finishing with a layer of pastry. Dust with icing sugar and serve immediately.

---

1 **Quick Raspberry Tarts**

Lightly whip 300 ml (½ pint) double cream in a bowl with a hand-held electric whisk until it forms soft peaks, then spoon into 6 x 8 cm (3½ inch) shop-bought sweet pastry cases. Top with 250 g (8 oz) raspberries and dust with icing sugar. Serve immediately.

2 **Individual Raspberry Millefeuilles** Unroll a 375 g (12 oz) pack chilled ready-rolled puff pastry and cut into 12 x 8 cm (3½ inch) squares. Place on a baking sheet and bake in a preheated oven, 220°C (425°F), Gas Mark 7, for 12–15 minutes until golden. Leave to cool. Meanwhile, lightly whip 300 ml

(½ pint) double cream in a bowl with a hand-held electric whisk until it forms soft peaks. Spoon the cream over 6 pieces of the pastry, then divide 250 g (8 oz) raspberries between the squares. Top with the remaining pastry and dust with icing sugar. Serve immediately.

3 Banana and Sticky Toffee Tarte Tatin

Serves 6

butter, for greasing

375 g (12 oz) pack chilled ready-rolled puff pastry

4 ripe bananas, cut in half lengthways

150 ml (¼ pint) shop-bought toffee sauce

vanilla ice cream or single cream, to serve (optional)

- Lightly grease a 23 cm (9 inch) round cake tin or frying pan with an ovenproof handle. Unroll the pastry and cut out a circle slightly larger than the tin or pan.

- Lay the bananas, cut side down, in the base of the tin or pan. Spoon over the toffee sauce, covering the bananas evenly. Place the pastry circle over the tin or pan, tucking the edges loosely round the edges so that steam can escape.

- Place in a preheated oven, 200°C (400°F), Gas Mark 6, for 20–25 minutes or until the pastry is puffed and golden. Leave to stand for a few minutes to cool slightly.

- Using an oven glove, place a serving dish on top of the tin or pan and turn upside down. Scrape any remaining sauce over the tarte tatin. Serve immediately with vanilla ice cream or single cream, if using.

 Banana Waffles with Toffee Sauce and Pecans Lightly toast 6 waffles and place in bowls. Slice 6 large bananas and arrange over the top of the waffles, then pour over 300 ml (½ pint) warmed shop-bought toffee sauce. Sprinkle over 25 g (1 oz) chopped pecans. Serve immediately with scoops of vanilla ice cream.

 Baked Bananas with Toffee Sauce Cook 6 large unpeeled bananas in an ovenproof dish in a preheated oven, 180°C (350°F), Gas Mark 4, for 15–20 minutes or until the skins have blackened and the flesh is soft. Slice the bananas lengthways, keeping them in their skins, and place in bowls. Drizzle over 300 ml (½ pint) warmed shop-bought toffee sauce, sprinkle each with some chopped pecans and serve with a scoop of vanilla ice cream.

DES-ENTE-LYI

30 Brandy Snaps with Limoncello Cream

Serves 6

sunflower oil, for greasing
75 g (3 oz) unsalted butter
75 g (3 oz) caster sugar
3 tablespoons golden syrup
75 g (3 oz) plain flour
1 teaspoon ground ginger
2 tablespoons brandy
1 tablespoon lemon juice

For the limoncello cream

200 ml (7 fl oz) double cream
3 tablespoons limoncello liqueur

- Lightly oil the handles of several wooden spoons and line 4 large baking sheets with nonstick baking paper.

- Place the butter, sugar and golden syrup in a heavy-based saucepan and warm gently over a medium heat until the mixture is combined. Leave to cool for 2–3 minutes, then stir in the flour, ginger, brandy and lemon juice. Mix until smooth.

- Place tablespoons of the mixture on to the prepared baking sheets, leaving plenty of room for spreading, to make 12–16 biscuits. Place 2 sheets at a time in a preheated oven, 190°C (375°F), Gas Mark 5, for 8–10 minutes or until golden.

- Leave to cool on the sheets for 10–15 seconds, then loosen a biscuit with a palette knife and roll around a spoon handle. Transfer to a wire rack to harden. Repeat with the remaining biscuits, returning to the oven for a few moments to soften if they set too hard.

- Lightly whip the cream and limoncello in a bowl with a hand-held electric whisk and spoon or pipe into the brandy snaps. Serve immediately.

1 Limoncello Brandy Snap Baskets

Make the limoncello cream as above. Place 6 shop-bought brandy snap baskets on plates and fill with the lemon cream. Top with 150 g (5 oz) raspberries and serve immediately.

2 Chocolate-dipped Limoncello Brandy

Snaps Melt 50 g (2 oz) plain dark or milk chocolate, broken into small pieces, in a heatproof bowl set over a saucepan of gently simmering water. Remove from the heat and dip each end of 12 shop-bought brandy snaps into the melted chocolate. Transfer to a wire rack to set. Make the limoncello cream as above. Once set, fill the brandy snaps with the cream and serve 2 per person.

Banana and Irish Cream Trifles

Serves 4

200 g (7 oz) mascarpone cheese

6 tablespoons Irish cream liqueur

200 g (7 oz) shop-bought banana loaf cake, cubed

3 bananas, sliced

4 tablespoons shop-bought toffee sauce

350 g (11½ oz) shop-bought fresh vanilla custard

25 g (1 oz) pecan nuts, chopped

- Beat together the mascarpone and 2 tablespoons of the liqueur in a bowl and chill.

- Meanwhile, divide the cake between 4 glasses, then drizzle each with 1 tablespoon of the liqueur. Add the bananas, reserving 4 slices for decoration, then drizzle each with ½ tablespoon of the toffee sauce. Spoon over the custard and top with the mascarpone cream.

- Drizzle with the remaining toffee sauce and decorate with the reserved banana slices and pecans. Serve immediately.

Banana, Irish Cream and Toffee Pudding

Slice 250 g (8 oz) shop-bought banana loaf cake and arrange in the base of a 900 ml (1½ pint) ovenproof dish. Drizzle over 2 tablespoons Irish cream liqueur. Top with 2 sliced bananas and 25 g (1 oz) chopped pecans, then pour over 250 ml (8 fl oz) shop-bought toffee sauce. Place in a preheated oven, 180°C (350°F), Gas Mark 4, for 15 minutes or until bubbling.

Banana and Irish Cream Custard

Pour 300 ml (½ pint) milk into a saucepan and place over a medium heat. Add a split vanilla pod and bring the milk to the boil. Place 3 egg yolks, 1 tablespoon cornflour and 2 tablespoons caster sugar in a heatproof bowl and whisk with a hand-held electric whisk until pale and thick. Strain the hot milk on to the egg mixture, whisking continuously until well combined. Return to the pan and heat gently over a low heat, stirring continuously, until thick enough to coat the back of a spoon. Slice the bananas into the custard and stir to combine. Stir in 2 tablespoons Irish cream liqueur. Pour the hot banana custard into 4 bowls and serve hot or cold, sprinkled with some chopped pecans and grated chocolate.

3 Chocolate Cups with Mint Syllabub

Serves 6

150 g (5 oz) plain dark chocolate, broken into small pieces
mint leaves, to decorate
cocoa powder, for dusting

For the mint syllabub

75 ml (3 fl oz) crème de menthe liqueur
25 g (1 oz) caster sugar
1 tablespoon lime juice
300 ml (½ pint) double cream

· To make the chocolate cups, melt the chocolate in a heatproof bowl set over a saucepan of gently simmering water. Draw 6 x 12 cm (5 inch) circles on greaseproof paper and cut out 1 cm (½ inch) outside the lines. (Do not use baking paper, as the chocolate will run too much).

· Place 6 upturned narrow tumblers or cups on a baking sheet. Spoon half the melted chocolate onto 3 of the greaseproof circles. Using a teaspoon, spread the chocolate within the drawn circles, making an attractive fluted edge.

· Lift each circle over a tumbler so that it falls loosely around the sides. Repeat to make 3 more baskets. Chill for 15–20 minutes until firm. Carefully remove the greaseproof paper and chill the baskets again.

· Meanwhile, to make the mint syllabub, place the liqueur, sugar and lime juice in a bowl and beat with a hand-held electric whisk, then whisk in the cream until it forms soft peaks.

· Spoon the syllabub into the chilled chocolate cups and serve immediately, decorated with mint leaves and dusted with a little cocoa powder.

---

1 Quick Chocolate and Mint Syllabubs

Crush 6 plain chocolate digestives and divide between 6 glasses. Make the mint syllabub as above, then spoon over the biscuits. Serve topped with a little grated plain chocolate and serve immediately.

2 White Chocolate and Peppermint Mousse Melt 250 g (8 oz) white chocolate, broken into small pieces, in a heatproof bowl set over a saucepan of gently simmering water, then leave to cool slightly. Lightly whip 225 ml (7½ fl oz) double cream in a bowl with a hand-held electric whisk until it forms soft peaks. Stir in

¼–½ teaspoon peppermint extract. Whisk 2 egg whites in a clean bowl with a hand-held electric whisk until they form soft peaks. Stir a little of the melted chocolate into the cream mixture, then fold in the rest of the chocolate mixture and egg whites. Spoon into 6 glasses and place in the freezer for 5–10 minutes before serving.

30 Portuguese Custard Tarts

Serves 8

1 tablespoon custard powder
25 g (1 oz) caster sugar
4 egg yolks
200 ml (7 fl oz) milk
grated rind of 1 lemon
200 ml (7 fl oz) crème fraîche
½ teaspoon vanilla extract
375 g (12 oz) pack chilled
   ready-rolled puff pastry
½ teaspoon ground cinnamon
4 tablespoons shop-bought
   caramel sauce, to serve

- Place the custard powder, sugar and egg yolks in a bowl, then add a little of the milk and stir to form a smooth paste. Whisk in the remaining milk, then pour into a saucepan and add the lemon rind and crème fraîche.

- Cook over a medium heat, whisking continuously, for 3–4 minutes until the custard has thickened. Remove from the heat and whisk in the vanilla extract. Leave to cool slightly.

- Unroll the pastry and cut out 8 circles using an 8 cm (3½ inch) cutter, re-rolling the trimmings if necessary. Push into 8 holes of a 12-hole nonstick muffin tin, pinching up the edges of the pastry.

- Pour the custard into the pastry shells until nearly full. Place in a preheated oven, 200°C (400°F), Gas Mark 6, for 15–20 minutes or until the pastry is golden and the filling puffed up. Leave to cool in the tin for a few minutes.

- Turn out the tarts on to serving plates, drizzle over the caramel sauce and serve immediately.

10 Quick Creamy Custard

Pour a 410 g (13 oz) can evaporated milk into a saucepan and stir in 1 teaspoon vanilla extract and 2 tablespoons caster sugar. Blend 2 tablespoons custard powder with 4 tablespoons cold water in a bowl to form a paste. Add the custard paste to the pan and cook over a low heat, whisking continuously, until the custard has boiled and thickened. Serve poured over crumbles and pies.

20 Nutmeg and Custard Tarts

Heat 300 ml (½ pint) single cream in a saucepan until lukewarm. Place 3 egg yolks and 50 g (2 oz) caster sugar in a heatproof bowl and beat with a hand-held electric whisk until creamy, then whisk in the warm cream. Strain into a jug. Place 8 x 8 cm (3½ inch) shop-bought sweet pastry cases on a baking sheet and pour in the custard. Sprinkle with grated nutmeg and place in a preheated oven, 180°C (350°F), Gas Mark 4, for 12–15 minutes or until set.

Mini Baked Alaskas

Serves 6

6 slices of shop-bought Madeira cake, cut into 1 cm (½ inch) thick slices

75 g (3 oz) raspberries

1 tablespoon icing sugar

1 tablespoon sherry (optional)

6 scoops of vanilla ice cream

4 egg whites

200 g (7 oz) caster sugar

- Line a baking sheet with nonstick baking paper. Using a 7 cm (3 inch) cutter, stamp out the Madeira cake to make 6 circles and place on the baking sheet.

- Place the raspberries, icing sugar and sherry, if using, in a bowl and roughly mash with a fork. Spoon the crushed raspberries and any juice evenly over the top of the cake circles. Place a scoop of ice cream on top of each cake, then place in the freezer while you make the meringue.

- Whisk the egg whites in a clean large bowl with a hand-held electric whisk until stiff, then gradually whisk in the sugar until the mixture is thick and glossy.

- Remove the sponge bases from the freezer, then quickly cover the ice cream and sponge with the meringue. Place in a preheated oven, 220°C (425°F), Gas Mark 7, for 3–4 minutes or until the meringue has browned. Serve immediately.

 Raspberry and Ice Cream Baked Meringue Puddings Divide 450 g (14½ oz) raspberries between 6 x 250 ml (8 fl oz) ramekins or ovenproof dishes. Whisk 3 large egg whites in a clean bowl with a hand-held electric whisk until stiff, then gradually whisk in 150 g (5 oz) caster sugar until the mixture is thick and glossy. Place 1 scoop of vanilla ice cream in each dish and cover with the meringue. Place on a baking sheet and bake in a preheated oven, 220°C (425°F), Gas Mark 7, for 3–4 minutes or until browned. Serve immediately.

 Chocolate and Raspberry Baked Alaska Line a 600 ml (1 pint) pudding mould with clingfilm and spoon in 500 g (1 lb) good-quality, slightly softened chocolate ice cream. Scatter with 125 g (4 oz) raspberries and spoon over 2 tablespoons shop-bought Belgian chocolate sauce. Cover with 3 halved shop-bought chocolate brownies and press down. Place in the freezer for 20 minutes until firm. Meanwhile, whisk 3 egg whites in a clean bowl with a hand-held electric whisk until stiff, then gradually whisk in 125 g (4 oz) caster sugar until the mixture is thick and glossy. Turn out the ice cream bombe on to an ovenproof plate, remove the clingfilm and cover with the meringue. Place in a preheated oven, 220°C (425°F), Gas Mark 7, for 3–4 minutes or until the meringue has browned. Serve immediately.

30 Coconut and Lime Jellies

Serves 4

135 g (4½ oz) pack lime jelly,
cut into small pieces
100 ml (3½ fl oz) boiling water
finely grated rind and juice of
2 limes
400 ml (14 fl oz) can coconut
milk, chilled
¼ coconut, white flesh cut into
thin slithers, to serve

- Place the jelly in a heatproof jug and pour over the measurement water. Stir until it is fully dissolved. Stir in the lime rind and juice, then whisk in the coconut milk.

- Pour into 4 x 150 ml (¼ pint) metal pudding moulds, cover with clingfilm and place in the freezer for 25 minutes until set. If not serving immediately, remove the jellies from the freezer and place in the refrigerator.

- Meanwhile, place the coconut in a frying pan and dry-fry over a medium heat until golden.

- To turn out the jellies, dip the base of the tins in warm water and invert on to serving plates. Serve with the toasted coconut.

 Lime and Coconut Creams

Place a 165 ml (5½ fl oz) can creamed coconut, the grated rind and juice of 1 lime, 250 g (8 oz) fat-free Greek yogurt and 25 g (1 oz) icing sugar in a bowl and whisk together. Spoon into 4 glasses and serve immediately.

 Coconut and Lime Sponge Puddings

Place 50 g (2 oz) caster sugar, 50 g (2 oz) softened unsalted butter and the finely grated rind of 1 lime in a bowl and beat together with a hand-held electric whisk until light and fluffy. Beat in 1 egg and the juice of 1 lime. Gently fold in 75 g (3 oz) self-raising flour and 50 g (2 oz) desiccated coconut. Spoon into 4 greased holes of a 6-hole nonstick muffin tin and place in a preheated oven, 180°C (350°F), Gas Mark 4, for 12–15 minutes until risen and golden. Serve with custard.

3 Orange and Rosemary Polenta Cake

Serves 6–8

175 g (6 oz) unsalted butter,
 softened
175 g (6 oz) caster sugar
finely grated rind and juice of
 1 orange
150 g (5 oz) ground almonds
2 large eggs
75 g (3 oz) coarse polenta
½ teaspoon baking powder

For the orange syrup

grated rind and juice of
 1 large orange
50 g (2 oz) caster sugar
2 tablespoons water
1 tablespoon chopped rosemary

- Line a 20 cm (8 inch) round cake tin with nonstick baking paper. Place the butter, sugar and orange rind in a large bowl and beat with a hand-held electric whisk until light and fluffy. Add the ground almonds and eggs and beat well. Stir in the orange juice, polenta and baking powder and mix until well combined.

- Spoon the mixture into the prepared cake tin and place in a preheated oven, 180°C (350°F), Gas Mark 4, for 20–25 minutes until risen and firm to the touch.

- Meanwhile, place all the syrup ingredients in a saucepan and bring to the boil. Reduce the heat and simmer for 2–3 minutes.

- Spoon the syrup over the cake in the tin, then turn out and serve in slices.

 1 Oranges in Rosemary Syrup

Place 200 g (7 oz) caster sugar, 200 ml (7 fl oz) water and 1 rosemary sprig in a saucepan and bring to the boil, stirring until the sugar has dissolved. Reduce the heat and simmer for 5 minutes. Cool slightly, then strain the syrup over 6 peeled and sliced oranges.

 2 Orange Polenta Sponges

Place 75 g (3 oz) softened unsalted butter, 75 g (3 oz) caster sugar and the finely grated rind of ½ orange in a bowl and beat with a hand-held electric whisk until light and fluffy, then beat in 50 g (2 oz) ground almonds, 1 egg, 100 g (3½ oz) coarse polenta and ½ teaspoon baking powder. Spoon into a greased and base-lined 6-hole nonstick muffin tin and place in a preheated oven, 180°C, (350°F), Gas Mark 4, for 12–15 minutes until risen and firm to the touch. Meanwhile, make the orange syrup as above. Remove the sponges from the muffin tin and spoon over the syrup to serve.

 # Meringues with Rosewater and Pomegranate

Serves 6

200 ml (7 fl oz) double cream
2 teaspoons rosewater
2 tablespoons icing sugar
a few drops of pink food
    colouring (optional)
6 meringue nests
50 g (2 oz) pomegranate seeds
25 g (1 oz) pistachio nuts,
    roughly chopped

- Place the cream, rosewater, icing sugar and food colouring, if using, in a bowl and whisk together with a hand-held electric whisk until it forms soft peaks.

- Spoon the cream into the meringue nests, then sprinkle each with a handful of the pomegranate seeds. Scatter over the pistachios and serve.

 ## Rosewater and Pomegranate Eton Mess

Place 450 ml (¾ pint) double cream, 2 teaspoons rosewater, 2 tablespoons icing sugar and a little pink food colouring (optional) in a bowl and whisk together with a hand-held electric whisk until it forms soft peaks. Gently stir in 8 roughly crushed meringue nests and 75 g (3 oz) pomegranate seeds, reserving a few for decoration. Pile into 6 glasses and decorate with the reserved pomegranate seeds and 50 g (2 oz) chopped pistachios. Chill for 10 minutes before serving.

 ## Pistachio and Rosewater Meringue Roulade

Whisk 5 egg whites in a clean large bowl with a hand-held electric whisk until stiff, then gradually whisk in 225 g (7½ oz) caster sugar until the mixture is thick and glossy. Gently fold in ½ teaspoon white wine vinegar, 1 teaspoon cornflour, ½ teaspoon vanilla extract and 50 g (2 oz) chopped pistachios. Spread the mixture into a 20 x 30 cm (8 x 12 inch) Swiss roll tin lined with nonstick baking paper. Place in the centre of a preheated oven, 180°C (350°F), Gas Mark 4, for 15 minutes. Leave to cool in the tin for 5 minutes. Turn out the meringue on to another piece of baking paper. Whip together 300 ml (½ pint) double cream, 2 teaspoons rosewater and 1 tablespoon icing sugar in a bowl with a hand-held electric whisk until it forms soft peaks. Spread evenly over the meringue and scatter over 75 g (3 oz) pomegranate seeds. Roll up the meringue, transfer to a serving plate and serve immediately.

DES-ENTE-TEO

30 Blackcurrant Galettes

Serves 4

375 g (12 oz) pack chilled
  ready-rolled puff pastry
15 g (½ oz) unsalted butter,
  melted
3 tablespoons granulated sugar
2 tablespoons chopped
  mint leaves
325 g (11 oz) blackcurrants,
  topped and tailed
double cream, to serve (optional)

- Unroll the pastry and cut out 4 x 10 cm (4 inch) rounds using a fluted cutter. Transfer to a baking sheet and prick with a fork, leaving a 1 cm (½ inch) border. Brush the melted butter over the edges of the pastry.

- Place the sugar and mint in a food processor and pulse to form a bright green sugar.

- Scatter the blackcurrants over the pastry circles within the borders, then sprinkle over half the mint sugar. Place in a preheated oven, 220°C (425°F), Gas Mark 7, for 15–20 minutes or until risen and golden.

- Sprinkle the galettes with the remaining mint sugar and serve with double cream, if using.

---

10 Blackcurrant and Cassis Coulis

Place 50 g (2 oz) caster sugar and 2 tablespoons crème de cassis in a saucepan. Stir in 125 g (4 oz) blackcurrants and heat gently until the sugar has dissolved. Simmer gently for 3–4 minutes until the fruit is soft. Place in a food processor or blender and blend to a purée, then press through a sieve into a bowl to remove the pips. Serve poured over ice cream or chopped fresh fruit.

20 Blackcurrant and Mint Fools

Place 450 g (14½ oz) blackcurrants, 100 g (3½ oz) caster sugar and 2 tablespoons crème de cassis in a large saucepan and simmer gently for 5–6 minutes until the fruit is soft. Place in a food processor or blender and blend to a purée, then press through a sieve into a bowl to remove the pips. Lightly whip 150 ml (¼ pint) double cream in a large bowl with a hand-held electric whisk until it forms soft peaks, then fold in 150 g (5 oz) Greek yogurt, 2 tablespoons chopped mint and the purée. Spoon into 4 glasses and serve immediately.

30 Lavender Crème Brûlées

Serves 6

3 egg yolks
1 tablespoon custard powder
3 tablespoons lavender sugar
300 ml (½ pint) milk
300 g (10 oz) mascarpone cheese
125 g (4 oz) caster sugar

- Chill 6 x 125 ml (4 fl oz) ramekins while you make the filling. Place the egg yolks, custard powder, lavender sugar and 3 tablespoons of the milk in a heatproof bowl and beat together.

- Meanwhile, warm the remaining milk in a saucepan. Gradually whisk into the egg mixture. Return to the pan and cook, whisking continuously, over a medium heat for 3–4 minutes until the mixture has thickened. Leave to cool slightly. Whisk in half of the mascarpone until smooth, then beat in the remaining mascarpone.

- Pour the mixture into the ramekins and place in the freezer for 15 minutes.

- Place the caster sugar in a small heavy-based saucepan over a low heat and leave until half of it has melted and started to colour, then gently stir it. Keep stirring until it has turned a deep golden caramel colour. Drizzle a little over the top of each ramekin. Leave to cool for a few minutes until the caramel has hardened, then serve.

 Quick Lavender and Fruit Crème Brûlées

Spoon 500 g (1 lb) shop-bought fruit compote, such as summer fruit, into 6 x 150 ml (¼ pint) ramekins. Spoon 750 g (1½ lb) Greek yogurt over the compote, then sprinkle the tops with 125 g (4 oz) lavender sugar. Place on a baking sheet and cook under a preheated hot grill for 4–5 minutes or until the sugar is brown and bubbling. Leave to stand for 3–4 minutes before serving.

Lavender Biscuits

Place 75 g (3 oz) plain flour, 50 g (2 oz) chilled diced unsalted butter and 25 g (1 oz) lavender sugar in a food processor and pulse until the mixture comes together to form a dough. Turn out on to a lightly floured surface and roll out to 5 mm (¼ inch) thick, then cut into 12 rounds using a 4 cm (1¾ inch) fluted cutter. Place on a baking sheet lined with nonstick baking paper and bake in a preheated oven, 180°C (350°F), Gas Mark 4, for 10–12 minutes. Serve 2 biscuits per person with Greek yogurt.

20 Hot Mango and Passion Fruit Soufflés

Serves 6

butter, for greasing
50 g (2 oz) caster sugar, plus
   2 tablespoons for dusting
100 ml (3½ fl oz) canned
   mango purée
3 passion fruit, pulp strained
   to remove the seeds
1 tablespoon cornflour
2 tablespoons cold water
icing sugar, for dusting

For the meringue

5 egg whites
75 g (3 oz) caster sugar

- Grease 6 x 200 ml (7 fl oz) ramekins or soufflé dishes, then dust with the 2 tablespoons sugar to cover the base and sides. Place on a baking sheet.

- Place the mango, passion fruit and the 50 g (2 oz) sugar in a saucepan over a low heat and stir until the sugar has dissolved, then bring to the boil. Blend the cornflour with the measurement water in a bowl to form a paste. Add to the mango in the pan and cook for 1 minute, stirring continuously. Pour into a large bowl and chill.

- Meanwhile, whisk the egg whites in a clean large bowl with a hand-held electric whisk until stiff, then gradually whisk in the sugar until the mixture is thick and glossy. Gently fold the meringue into the chilled mango.

- Spoon into the prepared dishes and spread the tops level, then clean the edges with a fingertip. Place in a preheated oven, 180°C (350°F), Gas Mark 4, for 10–12 minutes or until risen and golden. Dust with icing sugar and serve immediately.

10 Passion Fruit Syrup

Place 225 g (7½ oz) caster sugar, 250 ml (8 fl oz) water and the seeds and pulp of 6 passion fruit in a saucepan and cook over a low heat, stirring, until the sugar has dissolved. Increase the heat and allow the mixture to boil for 5–6 minutes until syrupy. Serve poured over mango sorbet.

30 Passion Fruit and Mango Millefeuille

Brush 3 large sheets of filo pastry with 25 g (1 oz) melted unsalted butter to stick them together, then cut into 12 x 12 x 5 cm (5 x 2 inch) rectangles. Place on a baking sheet and cook in preheated oven, 180°C (350°F), Gas Mark 4, for 5–7 minutes or until golden. Transfer to a cooling rack and leave to cool for 10 minutes. Meanwhile, lightly whip 200 ml (7 fl oz) double cream in a bowl with a hand-held electric whisk until it forms soft peaks, then stir in the pulp of 2 passion fruit and 3 tablespoons canned mango purée. Transfer to a bowl and chill for 10 minutes. Spoon the cream on to 6 of the filo rectangles, then top with the remaining pastry rectangles. Dust with icing sugar before serving.

3O Mini Baked Cappuccino Cheesecakes

Serves 6

75 g (3 oz) amaretti biscuits, crushed

25 g (1 oz) unsalted butter, melted

2 teaspoons espresso powder

2 tablespoons boiling water

75 g (3 oz) caster sugar

1 teaspoon vanilla extract

200 g (7 oz) light cream cheese

1 tablespoon cornflour

2 eggs

150 ml (¼ pint) whipping cream

cocoa powder, for dusting

- Line a 6-hole muffin tin with paper cases. Stir the crushed biscuits into the melted butter and press into the bases of the cases. Chill while you make the filling.

- Place the espresso powder in a heatproof bowl and pour over the measurement water to dissolve. Leave to cool.

- Place the sugar, vanilla extract, cream cheese, cornflour and eggs in a bowl and beat together until smooth, then stir in the espresso.

- Spoon the mixture over the biscuit bases and place in a preheated oven, 160°C (325°F), Gas Mark 3, for 15 minutes. Leave to cool in the tin for 5 minutes.

- Remove the cheesecakes from the cases and place on 6 serving plates. Lightly whip the cream in a bowl with a hand-held electric whisk until it forms soft peaks, then spoon on top of the warm cheesecakes. Dust with the cocoa powder and serve.

1O Coffee Meringues

Dissolve 2 teaspoons espresso powder in 2 tablespoons boiling water in a heatproof bowl and leave to cool. Lightly whip 300 ml (½ pint) double cream and the espresso in a bowl with a hand-held electric whisk until it forms soft peaks. Sandwich together 24 mini meringue shells with the coffee cream. Serve 2 meringues per person, dusted with cocoa powder.

2O Mascarpone and Coffee Creams

Dissolve 4 teaspoons espresso powder in 3 tablespoons boiling water in a heatproof bowl and leave to cool. Lightly crush 18 amaretti biscuits and divide half between 6 glasses. Place 300 g (10 oz) mascarpone cheese, 3 tablespoons icing sugar and the espresso in a bowl and beat with a hand-held electric whisk until smooth. Whisk in 300 ml (½ pint) double cream until creamy, then spoon into the glasses. Top with the remaining biscuits and serve.

Chocolate Zabaglione

Serves 6

50 g (2 oz) amaretti biscuits

2 tablespoons Marsala

For the zabaglione

25 g (1 oz) cocoa powder, sifted,
plus extra for dusting

5 egg yolks

50 g (2 oz) caster sugar

150 ml (¼ pint) Marsala

- Divide the biscuits between 6 tall-stemmed glasses. Spoon 1 teaspoon of the Marsala over each.

- To make the zabaglione, put the cocoa powder, egg yolks and sugar in a large heatproof bowl set over a saucepan of simmering water. Beat with a hand-held electric whisk until smooth, then gradually whisk in the remaining Marsala. Continue whisking for a further 8–10 minutes or until the mixture is slightly paler in colour, has increased in volume and is foamy.

- Carefully spoon the mixture into the glasses. Dust with cocoa powder and serve immediately.

 Sweet Marsala Creams

Place 4 tablespoons caster sugar, 1 egg and 1 extra egg yolk in a bowl and whisk with a hand-held electric whisk until it forms soft ribbons. Whisk in 250 g (8 oz) mascarpone cheese and 2 tablespoons Marsala. Lightly whip 250 ml (8 fl oz) whipping cream in a separate bowl with a hand-held electric whisk until it forms soft peaks, then fold into the mascarpone. Pour the cream mixture into 6 small glasses and scatter with 25 g (1 oz) grated plain dark chocolate. Serve with amaretti biscuits.

 Marsala and Chocolate Tart

Melt 200 g (7 oz) plain dark chocolate (85% cocoa solids), broken into small pieces, in a heatproof bowl set over a saucepan of gently simmering water, then leave to cool slightly. Place 2 large eggs, 50 g (2 oz) caster sugar and 3 tablespoons Marsala in a bowl and beat with a hand-held electric whisk until pale and fluffy. Whisk in the chocolate until well combined. Place a 20 cm (8 inch) shop-bought sweet pastry case on a baking sheet. Pour in the chocolate mixture and spread the top level. Place in a preheated oven, 160°C (325°F), Gas Mark 3, for about 10–12 minutes or until just set. The mixture should be slightly wobbly in the centre, but will continue to set on cooling. Leave to stand for 10 minutes, then serve with Marsala-flavoured double cream.

30 Parmesan and Rosemary Thins with Poached Grapes

Serves 6

200 ml (7 fl oz) Muscat
    sweet wine
100 ml (3½ fl oz) honey
500 g (l lb) seedless red grapes

For the biscuits

75 g (3 oz) plain flour, plus extra
    for dusting
50 g (2 oz) unsalted butter, diced
50 g (2 oz) Parmesan cheese,
    finely grated
1 teaspoon ground black pepper
½ teaspoon salt
1 tablespoon chopped rosemary

- To make the biscuits, place the flour in a bowl, add the butter and rub in with the fingertips until the mixture resembles fine breadcrumbs. Alternatively, use a food processor. Add the Parmesan, black pepper, salt and rosemary and mix in thoroughly. Bring the mixture together to form a dough.

- Turn the dough out on to a lightly floured surface and knead briefly. Roll out to 2 mm (⅛ inch) thick and cut out biscuits using a 6 cm (2½ inch) cutter. Place on to a large nonstick baking sheet and bake on the top shelf of a preheated oven, 160°C (325°F), Gas Mark 3, for 10 minutes. Carefully turn the biscuits over, then return to the oven for a further 5 minutes or until golden brown on both sides. Leave to cool on the sheet for 5 minutes, then turn out on to a wire rack to cool completely.

- Meanwhile, pour the wine into a small saucepan and add the honey. Bring to the boil, then reduce the heat and simmer for 10 minutes until syrupy. Add the grapes and simmer for 3–4 minutes. Leave to cool for 2 minutes.

- Spoon the grapes into 6 glasses and serve with the biscuits.

---

 1 Grape and Orange-blossom Honey

Fruit Salad Halve 500 g (1 lb) seedless red and green grapes and place in a bowl. Mix together 3 tablespoons orange-blossom honey and 3 tablespoons orange juice in a bowl, then pour over the grapes. Spoon into 6 small bowls and serve with spoonfuls of vanilla yogurt.

2 Grapes Poached in Rosemary Syrup

Place 100 g (3½ oz) caster sugar, 150 ml (¼ pint) water and 2 rosemary sprigs in a saucepan over a medium heat and bring to the boil, stirring until the sugar has dissolved. Reduce the heat and simmer for 5 minutes. Add 600 g (1 lb 3½ oz) seedless grapes and simmer gently for a further 5–10 minutes until soft. Remove the rosemary and serve the grapes with the syrup and Greek yogurt.

QuickCook
Healthy Options

Recipes listed by cooking time

30

20

10

Frozen Berry Yogurt Ice Cream

Serves 4

400 g (13 oz) frozen mixed
  summer berries
250 g (8 oz) fat-free
  Greek yogurt
2 tablespoons icing sugar
wafers, to serve

- Place half the berries, the yogurt and icing sugar in a food processor or blender and blend until fairly smooth and the berries have broken up.

- Add the rest of the berries and pulse until they are slightly broken up but some texture remains. Place scoops of the yogurt ice cream into bowls and serve immediately with wafers, if using.

 Frozen Berry Yogurt Ice Cream Sundaes Place 150 g (5 oz) raspberries and 1 tablespoon icing sugar in a food processor or blender and blend to make a smooth coulis, then sieve to remove the pips. Make the yogurt ice cream as above. Break up 4 meringue nests and divide half between 4 glasses. Add 1 scoop of the yogurt ice cream to each glass, then pour over a little of the coulis. Repeat the layers, finishing with the coulis. Serve immediately.

Frozen Berry Yogurt Ice Cream in Lemon Tuile Baskets Whisk 1 egg white in a clean bowl with a hand-held electric whisk until stiff, then gradually whisk in 50 g (2 oz) caster sugar until thick and glossy. Fold in 25 g (1 oz) cooled melted unsalted butter, the rind of ½ lemon and 25 g (1 oz) plain flour. Place 2 heaped teaspoons of the mixture, spaced well apart, on to each of 2 lightly greased nonstick baking sheets. Spread out to 12 cm (5 inch) rounds. Place one baking sheet at a time in a preheated oven, 180°C (350°F), Gas Mark 4, for 5–6 minutes or until golden around the edges. Carefully drape the biscuits over upturned oiled timbales to form baskets and leave to cool. Meanwhile, make the yogurt ice cream as above. Serve the tuile baskets filled with scoops of the ice cream.

20 Easy Blackberry Fool

Serves 4

300 g (10 oz) blackberries,
  plus extra to decorate
50 g (2 oz) icing sugar
1 tablespoon lemon juice
250 g (8 oz) fromage frais
200 g (7 oz) fat-free
  Greek yogurt

- Place the blackberries, icing sugar and lemon juice in a food processor or blender and blend to a purée, then press through a sieve into a large bowl to remove the pips. Beat in the fromage frais and yogurt.

- Spoon into 4 glass dishes and chill for 10 minutes. Decorate with extra blackberries before serving.

1 **Blackberry Coulis**
Place 250 g (8 oz) blackberries, 50 g (2 oz) golden caster sugar and 100 ml (3½ fl oz) water in a small saucepan and bring to the boil. Reduce the heat and simmer for 5 minutes until the fruit is soft. Stir in ½ teaspoon vanilla extract. Tip into a food processor or blender and blend to a purée, then press through a sieve into a bowl, rubbing it through with the back of a ladle or spoon. Serve warm or chilled with fat-free Greek yogurt.

3 **Blackberry Upside-down Cake**
Lightly grease and base-line a 20 cm (8 inch) loose-bottomed round cake tin with nonstick baking paper. Scatter 350 g (11½ oz) blackberries over the base and sprinkle over 2 tablespoons caster sugar. Place 2 eggs, 75 g (3 oz) caster sugar and the grated rind of 1 lemon in a large bowl and beat with a hand-held electric whisk until pale and thick and the whisk leaves a trail when lifted above the mixture. Gently stir in the juice of 1 lemon and fold in 75 g (3 oz) self-raising flour. Pour over the blackberries and place in a preheated oven, 180°C (350°F), Gas Mark 4, for 20–25 minutes or until golden brown and firm to the touch. Leave to cool in the tin for a few minutes, then invert on to a plate. Serve with fat-free fromage frais.

Griddled Peaches and Apricots with Honey Yogurt

Serves 4

2 tablespoons vanilla sugar

3 peaches, halved, stoned and
　cut into quarters

4 apricots, halved and stoned

200 g (7 oz) fat-free
　Greek yogurt

2 tablespoons clear honey

- Place the sugar in a large bowl, then add the fruit and toss gently to coat.

- Preheat a griddle pan until hot, then add the peaches, cut side down, and griddle over a medium heat for 2–3 minutes until caramelized, then add the apricots. Turn over the peaches and cook for a further 2–3 minutes or until the apricots and peaches are soft.

- Meanwhile, place the yogurt in a bowl and pour over the honey. Stir to create a rippled effect. Serve the warmed griddled fruit with the honey yogurt.

 Oven-roasted Cinnamon Peaches and Apricots Halve and stone 3 peaches and cut into quarters, then halve and stone 3 apricots and place cut side up in an ovenproof dish. Mix together 3 tablespoons soft light brown sugar and 1 teaspoon ground cinnamon in a bowl and sprinkle over the fruit. Place in a preheated oven, 200°C (400°F), Gas Mark 6, for 10–15 minutes or until softened and starting to caramelize. Serve with dollops of fat-free yogurt.

 Poached Vanilla Peaches Dunk 4 ripe peaches into a heatproof bowl of boiling water for 1 minute, then place in a bowl of cold water and slip off the skins. Place in a saucepan that holds them snugly, then pour over 200 ml (7 fl oz) water. Split open 1 vanilla pod and scrape out the seeds. Mix the seeds with 100 g (3½ oz) caster sugar in a bowl and sprinkle over the peaches, placing the vanilla pod in the middle. Cover with a lid and cook for 20–25 minutes, turning once and stirring to dissolve the sugar. Serve warm with some syrup poured over.

 # Carpaccio of Pineapple with Basil

Serves 4

1 supersweet pineapple, chilled
2 tablespoons honey
juice of ½ lime
2 teaspoons freshly ground
    black pepper
6 large basil leaves, shredded

- Cut the top and base off the pineapple. Hold the pineapple firmly, resting it on the cut base. Slice off the skin, working from top to bottom, removing any brown 'eyes'. Halve lengthways, remove the tough central core using an apple corer and cut into thin slices. Arrange on a large serving platter.

- Mix together the honey, lime juice and black pepper in a small bowl and drizzle over the pineapple. Scatter over the basil and serve immediately.

 ### Pineapple and Basil Sorbet

Place 450 g (14½ oz) frozen pineapple chunks, 2 tablespoons caster sugar and 2 tablespoons lime juice in a food processor and pulse until the pineapple starts to break down. Add 2 tablespoons freshly chopped basil and blitz for 2–3 minutes until the mixture starts to come together. Spoon into 4 bowls and serve immediately.

 ### Pineapple and Basil Skewers

Skin and core 1 pineapple as above and cut into 2.5 cm (1 inch) cubes. Place in a large bowl and stir in 3 tablespoons honey, 1 tablespoon freshly chopped basil and the grated rind and juice of 1 lime. Leave to marinate for 15 minutes, then thread on to 8 metal skewers. Cook under a preheated hot grill or on a barbecue for 3–4 minutes on each side or until lightly golden. Serve 2 kebabs per person.

Balsamic and Black Pepper Strawberries

Serves 4

500g (1 lb) strawberries, hulled and halved
2 tablespoons balsamic vinegar
1 teaspoon freshly ground black pepper

- Place the strawberries in a bowl and pour over the vinegar.
- Stir well, to incorporate the flavours, then add the black pepper to taste. Serve immediately.

 Strawberry and Black Pepper Sauce Place 500g (1 lb) hulled strawberries and 2 tablespoons icing sugar in a food processor or blender and blend until the sauce is smooth. Transfer to a jug and stir in 1–2 teaspoons freshly ground black pepper. Chill for 10 minutes, then serve poured over frozen yogurt.

 Baked Balsamic and Black Pepper Strawberry Parcels Mix together 700 g (1 lb 7 oz) hulled strawberries, 100 ml (3½ fl oz) balsamic vinegar, 25 g (1 oz) caster sugar and 1 teaspoon black pepper in a large bowl. Divide between 4 double thickness 25 cm (10 inch) foil squares, folding in the edges to seal. Place the parcels on a baking sheet and bake in a preheated oven, 160°C (325°F), Gas Mark 3, for 25 minutes.

1 Pistachio and Orange-blossom Oranges

Serves 4

4 large oranges

2–3 teaspoons orange-blossom water

1 tablespoon icing sugar

2 tablespoons pistachio nuts, roughly chopped

- Using a sharp knife, slice the top and bottom off the oranges, then remove the skin and pith. Slice each orange into 6 rounds, reserving the juice.

- Mix together the reserved juice, orange slices, orange-blossom water, to taste, and icing sugar in a bowl.

- Divide the orange slices between 4 bowls, then drizzle the juice over each and sprinkle with the pistachios.

2 Pistachio Meringues with Orange-blossom Water

Place 100 g (3½ oz) fromage frais, 1 teaspoon grated orange rind, 1 tablespoon icing sugar and ½–1 teaspoon orange-blossom water, to taste, in a bowl and stir together. Spoon the mixture into 4 meringue nests. Using a sharp knife, remove the skin and outer pith from 1 orange. Cut between the pith into segments. Top the meringues with a couple of the orange segments and sprinkle over 25 g (1 oz) chopped pistachios. Serve immediately.

3 Orange and Pistachio Risotto

Place 600 ml (1 pint) semi-skimmed milk, 50 g (2 oz) caster sugar and the grated rind of 1 orange in a small saucepan and heat gently to simmering point. Meanwhile, melt 25 g (1 oz) unsalted butter in a saucepan and stir in 175 g (6 oz) Arborio rice. Mix well to coat the grains in the butter, then add the juice of 1 orange. Bring to the boil, then reduce the heat and simmer for 2–3 minutes. Gradually add the warm milk to the rice, stirring occasionally, until most of it has been absorbed and the rice is slightly al dente with a creamy sauce. This should take about 20–25 minutes. Spoon into 4 bowls and serve sprinkled with 25 g (1 oz) chopped pistachios.

3 Spiced Dried Fruit Compote

Serves 4

4 ready-to-eat dried pears
  or apple rings
4 ready-to-eat dried figs
8 ready-to-eat dried apricots
8 ready-to-eat dried prunes
  (about 75 g/3 oz)
600 ml (1 pint) fresh orange juice
1 cinnamon stick
1 star anise
brown sugar, to taste

To serve (optional)
fat-free Greek yogurt
ground cinnamon

- Place the dried fruits in a saucepan with the orange juice and spices and bring to the boil. Reduce the heat, cover and simmer for 25–30 minutes until the fruits are plump and tender and the liquid syrupy.

- Check the liquid occasionally during cooking, adding a little water if necessary. Taste the liquid and add a little sugar if required. Remove the spices.

- Spoon into 4 bowls and serve with spoonfuls of fat-free Greek yogurt sprinkled with a little ground cinnamon, if liked.

 **Prune and Apple Compote**

Place 250 g (8 oz) ready-to-eat dried prunes and 300 ml (½ pint) apple juice in a saucepan and bring to the boil. Reduce the heat and simmer for 8–10 minutes until the prunes are plump and the liquid syrupy. Serve with fat-free Greek yogurt.

2 Tropical Fruit Compote

Place 50 g (2 oz) caster sugar, a strip of lemon peel and 600 ml (1 pint) cold water in a saucepan and bring to the boil, stirring until the sugar has dissolved, then boil the syrup for 10 minutes. Add 250 g (8 oz) dried tropical fruits (such as mango, pineapple, papaya and melon) to the pan and simmer gently for 5–6 minutes until the fruit is tender. Serve with a little shredded basil.

Ricotta with Warm Cinnamon Honey

Serves 4

500 g (1 lb) ricotta cheese
8 tablespoons honey
½ teaspoon ground cinnamon
handful of raspberries, to serve

- Line 4 x 125 ml (4 fl oz) dariole moulds with clingfilm. Press the ricotta into the moulds, then place in the freezer for 5 minutes.

- Meanwhile, gently warm the honey and cinnamon in a small saucepan.

- Remove the ricotta moulds from the freezer and invert on to plates. Remove the clingfilm and pour over the warm syrup. Serve with a few raspberries.

 Ricotta and Honey Baked Nectarines

Halve and stone 4 nectarines and place cut side up in an ovenproof dish. Place 125 g (4 oz) ricotta cheese, 2 tablespoons honey and ½ teaspoon ground cinnamon in a bowl and beat together. Pile the mixture on to the fruit and place in a preheated oven, 200°C (400°F), Gas Mark 6, for 10–15 minutes or until the fruit is soft. Drizzle with a little extra honey to serve.

 Baked Ricotta Cakes with Honey

Place 250 g (8 oz) ricotta cheese in a bowl and break it up with a wooden spoon. Whisk 2 egg whites in a clean bowl with a hand-held electric whisk until stiff, then fold into the ricotta with 4 tablespoons honey. Spoon the mixture into 4 greased 125 ml (4 fl oz) ramekins and spread the tops level. Place on a baking sheet and bake in a preheated oven, 180°C (350°F), Gas Mark 4, for 20 minutes or until risen and golden. Turn out the ricotta cakes on to serving plates and serve drizzled with 4 tablespoons warmed honey flavoured with a pinch of ground cinnamon.

DES-HEAL-QOE

10 Griddled Mango with Lime and Chilli Syrup

Serves 4

4 ripe mangoes

For the lime and chilli syrup

1 red chilli, deseeded and
  thinly sliced
grated rind and juice of 1 lime
125 g (4 oz) golden caster sugar
150 ml (¼ pint) cold water

- To make the lime and chilli syrup, place all the ingredients in a small saucepan and stir over a low heat until the sugar has dissolved. Bring to the boil, then reduce the heat and simmer for 8–10 minutes until syrupy.

- Meanwhile, heat a griddle pan. Using a sharp knife, remove the skins from the mangoes, then cut each one into thick slices either side of the stone. Place the mango slices on the hot griddle and cook for 4–5 minutes on each side.

- Transfer to 4 serving plates and serve with the warm syrup drizzled over the top.

2 Mango, Lime and Chilli Coulis

Peel, stone and cut 2 ripe mangoes into chunks, then place in a food processor or blender with 1 deseeded and chopped red chilli and the grated rind and juice of 2 limes. Blend for 4–5 minutes until smooth. Serve poured over frozen yogurt.

3 Mango Fruit Salad with Lime and

Chilli Syrup Prepare the syrup as above, transfer to a jug and chill for 10–12 minutes. Remove the skins from 2 ripe mangoes using a sharp knife, then cut each one into thin slices either side of the stone. Place in a bowl and pour over the cooled syrup.

DES-HEAL-BUW

20 Fluffy Lemon Mousse

Serves 4

150 g (5 oz) fat-free
  Greek yogurt
150 ml (¼ pint) half-fat
  crème fraîche
grated rind and juice of
  1 unwaxed lemon
50 g (2 oz) caster sugar
2 egg whites
grated lemon rind,
  to decorate

- Place the yogurt, crème fraîche, lemon rind and sugar in a large bowl and beat together with a hand-held electric whisk until smooth. Add the lemon juice and whisk again until the mixture has thickened slightly.

- Whisk the egg whites in a clean bowl with a hand-held electric whisk until they form soft peaks, then fold into the lemon mixture.

- Spoon the mousse into 4 glasses and chill for 10 minutes. Serve decorated with the lemon rind.

---

10 Homemade Creamy Lemon Yogurt

Mix together 500 g (1 lb) fat-free Greek yogurt and 4–6 tablespoons lemon curd, to taste, in a bowl. Spoon into 4 glasses and serve topped with 125 g (4 oz) crunchy granola.

30 Lemon Soufflés

Lightly grease 4 x 250 ml (8 fl oz) ramekins or soufflé dishes, then dust the insides with 2 tablespoons caster sugar. Place on a baking sheet. Finely grate the rind of 1 lemon and squeeze the juice of 2 lemons to make 100 ml (3½ fl oz). Place in a the lemon rind and juice in a saucepan with 50 g (2 oz) caster sugar and cook over a low heat until the sugar has dissolved, then bring to the boil. Blend 1 tablespoon cornflour and 2 tablespoons cold water in a bowl to form a paste. Add to the lemon mixture in the pan and cook for 1 minute, stirring continuously until thickened. Transfer to a bowl and chill for 10 minutes. Whisk 4 egg whites in a clean large bowl with a hand-held electric whisk until stiff, then gradually whisk in 50 g (2 oz) caster sugar until the mixture is thick and glossy. Gently fold the cooled lemon mixture into the meringue. Spoon the mixture into the prepared dishes and spread the tops level, then clean the edges with a fingertip. Place in a preheated oven, 180°C (350°F), Gas Mark 4, for 10–12 minutes until risen and golden. Serve immediately.

Mango, Cardamom and Mint Fools

Serves 6

625 g (1¼ lb) fat-free
  Greek yogurt, chilled
5 green cardamom pods,
  seeds finely crushed
2 tablespoons icing sugar
grated rind and juice of 1 lime
200 ml (7 fl oz) canned
  mango purée
2 tablespoons chopped mint

To decorate

chopped mango
mint sprigs

- Place the yogurt, crushed cardamom, icing sugar, lime rind and juice in a large bowl and slowly whisk together with a hand-held electric whisk for 1–2 minutes.

- Whisk in the mango pureé until combined, then stir in the mint. Spoon into 6 glasses and chill for 10 minutes.

- Serve decorated with chopped mango and a mint sprig.

 Simple Mango and Cardamom Fruit Salad Peel, stone and slice 4 mangoes and arrange on a plate. Sprinkle over the crushed powder from 4 green cardamom pods, then grate over the rind of 1 lime and squeeze over the juice. Sprinkle with 2 tablespoons chopped mint and serve immediately.

 Mango and Cardamom Upside-down Cake Lightly grease and base-line a 20 cm (8 inch) loose-bottomed round cake tin with nonstick baking paper. Arrange 2 peeled, stoned and sliced mangoes over the base and sprinkle with 1 tablespoon soft light brown sugar. Place 2 eggs and 75 g (3 oz) caster sugar in a bowl and beat with a hand-held electric whisk until pale and thick and the whisk leaves a trail when lifted above the mixture. Gently stir in the crushed powder from 4 green cardamom pods, the grated rind of 1 lime and 1 tablespoon lime juice. Fold in 75 g (3 oz) self-raising flour. Pour over the mangoes and place in a preheated oven, 180°C (350°F), Gas Mark 4, for 20–25 minutes or until golden brown and firm to the touch. Leave to cool in the tin for a few minutes, then invert on to a plate and serve warm.

30 Blackberry and Apple Puffs

Serves 6

2 tablespoons vegetable oil
75 g (3 oz) plain flour
½ tsp ground cinnamon
pinch of salt
50 g (2 oz) caster sugar,
  plus 1 tablespoon
200 ml (7 fl oz) milk
2 large eggs
125 g (4 oz) blackberries
1 small dessert apple, cored
  and cut into thin slices
icing sugar, for dusting

- Liberally brush a 12-hole bun tray with the oil. Place in a preheated oven, 180°C (350°F), Gas Mark 4 to heat.

- Meanwhile, sift the flour, cinnamon and salt into a large bowl. Stir in the 50 g (2 oz) sugar and make a well in the centre. Whisk together the milk and eggs in a jug, then gradually whisk into the flour to form a smooth batter.

- Remove the hot bun tin from the oven and pour in the batter. Add a couple of blackberries in the centres, then top with apple slices and sprinkle with the 1 tablespoon sugar.

- Return to the oven and cook for 20 minutes or until risen, golden and cooked through. Serve dusted with icing sugar.

 Blackberry Sauce Place 300 g (10 oz) blackberries, 2 tablespoons caster sugar and the grated rind and juice of 1 lemon in a saucepan and heat gently for 5–6 minutes until the fruit starts to burst. Serve warm with spoonfuls of vanilla yogurt.

 Puffed Apple and Blackberry Pancake Pudding Melt 25 g (1 oz) unsalted butter in a 20 cm (8 inch) frying pan with an ovenproof handle, add 4 sliced apples and cook for 2–3 minutes. Sprinkle over 1 tablespoon caster sugar and 1 tablespoon lemon juice, stirring gently until the sugar has dissolved. Meanwhile, mix together 100 g (3½ oz) plain flour and 1 tablespoon caster sugar in a large bowl and make a well in the centre. Whisk together 4 eggs and 175 ml (6 fl oz) milk in a jug, then gradually whisk into the flour to form a smooth batter. Pour over the apples, then scatter over 125 g (4 oz) blackberries. Place in a preheated oven, 220°C (425°F), Gas Mark 7, for 15–20 minutes or until puffed and golden. Serve immediately.

Banana and Buttermilk Pancakes

Serves 4

125 g (4 oz) plain flour
1 teaspoon baking powder
pinch of salt
200 ml (7 fl oz) buttermilk
1 egg
2 small bananas, thinly sliced
1 tablespoon vegetable oil,
  for frying

To serve

1 banana, sliced
25 g (1 oz) pecan nuts, chopped
1 tablespoon honey

- Sift the flour, baking powder and salt into a large bowl and make a well in the centre. Whisk together the buttermilk and egg in a jug, then gradually whisk into the flour mixture to form a smooth batter. Stir in the sliced bananas.

- Heat a large nonstick frying pan over a medium heat. Using a scrunched up piece of kitchen paper, dip into the oil and use to wipe over the pan. Drop 3 large tablespoons of the batter into the pan to make 3 pancakes, spreading the batter out slightly with a spoon. Cook for 2–3 minutes until bubbles start to appear on the surface and the underside is golden brown, then flip over and cook for a further 2 minutes. Remove from the pan and keep warm. Repeat with the remaining batter to make 8 pancakes.

- Serve the pancakes topped with extra sliced banana, sprinkled with pecans and drizzled with a little honey.

Instant Banana Pancakes

Warm 8 ready-made pancakes according to the packet instructions. Slice 4 bananas and divide between the pancakes. Fold them over and serve 2 pancakes per person drizzled with a little honey and a dollop of fat-free Greek yogurt.

Banana and Buttermilk Muffins

Sift 275 g (9 oz) plain flour and 1 tablespoon baking powder into a bowl and stir in 125 g (4 oz) caster sugar. In another bowl, beat together 2 mashed bananas, 1 large egg, 250 ml (8 fl oz) buttermilk and 100 g (3½ oz) melted unsalted butter. Stir the wet ingredients into the dry ingredients until just combined, then spoon the mixture into a greased 12-hole nonstick muffin tin. Place in a preheated oven, 190°C (375°F), Gas Mark 5, for 20 minutes or until risen and firm to the touch. Remove from the tin and serve warm with a drizzle of honey and fat-free yogurt.

30 Clementine Upside-down Cake

Serves 4–6

butter, for greasing

4 clementines, peeled and
cut into 5 slices

4 tablespoons orange and
ginger marmalade

2 eggs

75 g (3 oz) caster sugar

finely grated rind and juice
of 1 clementine

75 g (3 oz) self-raising flour

fromage frais, to serve (optional)

- Lightly grease and base-line a 20 cm (8 inch) loose-bottomed round cake tin with nonstick baking paper. Arrange the clementine slices over the base and spoon over the marmalade.

- Place the eggs and sugar in a bowl and beat with a hand-held electric whisk until pale and thick and the whisk leaves a trail when lifted above the mixture. Gently stir in the clementine rind and juice and fold in the flour.

- Pour over the clementines and place in a preheated oven, 180°C (350°F), Gas Mark 4, for 20–25 minutes or until golden brown and firm to the touch. Leave to cool in the tin for a few minutes.

- Invert the tin on to a plate and serve the cake in slices with dollops of fromage frais, if using.

1 Ginger Pan-roasted Clementines

Peel 8 clementines and cut into quarters. Place 100 g (3½ oz) caster sugar and 1 teaspoon ground ginger in a frying pan over a high heat, add the clementines and cook for 5 minutes until caramelized. Stir in 2 tablespoons orange juice. Cool slightly and serve with fat-free Greek yogurt.

2 Clementine Yogurt Whip

Finely grate the rind from 1 clementine and squeeze the juice into a bowl. Whisk in 300 g (10 oz) fat-free Greek yogurt and 1 tablespoon icing sugar. Peel and roughly chop 3 clementines and stir half into the yogurt mixture. Stir in 2 broken meringue nests. Spoon into 4 glasses and top with the remaining chopped clementines, to serve.

3 0 Trio of Grapefruits with Ginger Syrup

Serves 4

2 pink grapefruits
2 red grapefruits
2 white grapefruits
2 tablespoons chopped mint

For the ginger syrup

125 g (4 oz) caster sugar
2 pieces of stem ginger in syrup,
  finely chopped
2 tablespoons stem ginger syrup
  (taken from the jar)

- Remove the skin from the grapefruits then, holding over a bowl to collect the juice, use a sharp knife to cut into segments between the pith. Place the segments in a serving bowl and chill.

- To make the ginger syrup, pour the grapefruit juice into a jug to make 200 ml (7 fl oz), then place in a saucepan with the sugar, stem ginger and stem ginger syrup. Bring to the boil, then reduce the heat and simmer for 8–10 minutes. Transfer to a heatproof jug and chill for 10 minutes to cool.

- Pour the cooled syrup over the grapefruit and stir in the mint. Serve immediately.

 Grilled Grapefruit with Ginger and Mint Cut 2 pink or red grapefruits in half and place on a baking sheet cut sides up. Chop 2 pieces of stem ginger in syrup into small pieces and scatter over the top, then drizzle over 1 tablespoon stem ginger syrup. Cook under a preheated medium grill for 5 minutes or until the grapefruit is golden. Serve immediately with chopped mint and a dollop of fat-free Greek yogurt.

 Grapefruit Salad with Warm Ginger Syrup Drain 2 x 540 g (1 lb 1½ oz) cans grapefruit segments in juice and place in a bowl, reserving 200 ml (7 fl oz) of the juice. Make the ginger syrup as above using the reserved canned juice. Cool slightly, then pour over the grapefruit. Serve immediately.

Floating Islands with Elderflower Cordial and Berries

Serves 6

625 g (1¼ lb) frozen mixed
   summer berries
150 g (5 oz) caster sugar
4 tablespoons elderflower cordial

For the floating islands

2 large egg whites
pinch of salt
50 g (2 oz) caster sugar

- Place the berries, sugar and cordial in a saucepan and cook over a low heat, stirring, until the sugar has dissolved. Simmer for 4–5 minutes until the berries have softened, but still retain their shape.

- To make the floating islands, fill a large frying pan with water and bring to a simmer. Whisk the egg whites and salt in a clean bowl with a hand-held electric whisk until they form soft peaks, then gradually whisk in the sugar until the mixture is thick and glossy.

- Drop 6 heaped tablespoons of the meringue mixture into the simmering water, using a spoon to help it slide off. Turn after 30 seconds using a slotted spoon and cook for another 30 seconds. Remove and drain on kitchen paper.

- Spoon the warm berries and the juice into 6 serving bowls and float a meringue on top.

 Light Elderflower Cream

Place 300 g (10 oz) fat-free fromage frais in a bowl and stir in 2 tablespoons elderflower cordial and 1 tablespoon icing sugar. Serve poured over sliced fresh fruit.

 Poached Nectarines or Peaches in Elderflower Pressé

Dunk 6 whole nectarines or peaches into a heatproof bowl of boiling water for 1 minute, then place in a bowl of cold water and slip off the skins. Place 450 ml (¾ pint) elderflower pressé and 75 g (3 oz) caster sugar in a saucepan that will hold the fruit snugly. Bring to the boil, stirring until the sugar has dissolved. Add the fruit, cover and simmer gently for 10 minutes. Turn the fruit and poach for a further 10 minutes until just tender. Spoon the nectarines or peaches into 6 bowls and pour over the syrup, to serve.

Watermelon with Mint Sugar

Serves 4

1 kg (2 lb) watermelon

4 tablespoons golden
 caster sugar

20 g (¾ oz) mint leaves

- Remove the skin from the watermelon and cut the flesh into cubes, discarding any seeds. Divide between 4 plates.

- Place the sugar and mint in a food processor and pulse to form a bright green sugar.

- Serve the watermelon sprinkled with the mint sugar.

---

2 Watermelon and Mint Kebabs

Remove the skin and seeds from 1 kg (2 lb) watermelon, cut into 2.5 cm (1 inch) cubes and thread on to 8 metal skewers. Make the mint sugar as above, then sprinkle over the kebabs. Griddle or grill the kebabs for 3–4 minutes on each side. Serve 2 kebabs per person.

3 Watermelon, Lime and Mint Salad

Remove the skin and seeds from 1 kg (2 lb) watermelon, cut into cubes and place in a large bowl. Drizzle with the juice of 2 limes and 2 teaspoons grated lime rind. Leave to infuse for 20 minutes. Make the mint sugar as above and serve with the fruit salad.

Baked Red Fruit and Hazelnut Meringues

Serves 4

2 large egg whites
100 g (3½ oz) caster sugar
25 g (1 oz) ground toasted
  hazelnuts
350 g (11½ oz) strawberries,
  hulled and halved
350 g (11½ oz) raspberries

- Whisk the egg whites in a clean bowl with a hand-held electric whisk until they form soft peaks, then gradually whisk in the sugar until the mixture is thick and glossy. Gently fold in the hazelnuts.

- Mix together the strawberries and the raspberries in a bowl and divide between 4 x 250 ml (8 fl oz) ramekins or ovenproof dishes. Pile the meringue on top of each.

- Place on a baking sheet and bake in a preheated oven, 200°C (400°F), Gas Mark 6, for 7 minutes or until the meringues are browned. Serve immediately.

Red Fruit Meringue Creams

Break up 2 meringue nests and place in the bottom of 4 glasses. Place 125 g (4 oz) raspberries and 125 g (4 oz) hulled and sliced strawberries in a bowl and sprinkle over 1 tablespoon caster sugar. Crush the fruit slightly with a fork, then spoon over the meringue. Mix together 200 g (7 oz) half-fat crème fraîche, 200 ml (7 fl oz) fat-free Greek yogurt and 1 tablespoon caster sugar in a bowl, then stir in 2 crushed meringue nests. Spoon on top of the fruit and serve immediately.

Hazelnut and Raspberry Meringue Roulade

Whisk 5 egg whites in a clean large bowl with a hand-held electric whisk until stiff, then gradually whisk in 225 g (7½ oz) caster sugar until the mixture is thick and glossy. Gently fold in ½ teaspoon white wine vinegar, 50 g (2 oz) ground toasted hazelnuts and 1 teaspoon cornflour. Spread the mixture into a 20 x 30 cm (8 x 12 inch) Swiss roll tin lined with nonstick baking paper. Place in the centre of a preheated oven, 180°C (350°F), Gas Mark 4, for 15 minutes. Leave to cool in the tin for 5 minutes. Turn out the meringue on to another piece of baking paper. Mix together 200 g (7 oz) fat-free Greek yogurt, 200 ml (7 fl oz) half-fat crème fraîche and 2 tablespoons caster sugar in a bowl. Spread evenly over the meringue and sprinkle with 150 g (5 oz) raspberries. Roll up the meringue and serve immediately.

10 Pineapple and Mint Salad

Serves 4

1 ripe pineapple
3 tablespoons chopped mint
grated rind and juice of 1 lime
1 red chilli, deseeded and finely
   chopped (optional)

- Cut the top and base off the pineapple. Hold the pineapple firmly, resting it on the cut base. Slice off the skin, working from top to bottom, removing any brown 'eyes'. Cut into quarters lengthways, remove the tough central core and cut into cubes.

- Place in a large bowl and stir in the mint, lime rind and juice and chilli, if using. Stir well to combine and serve immediately.

2 Pineapple and Mint Salsa

Slice the skin from 1 pineapple as above, then cut into 1 cm (½ inch) thick rounds and remove the tough central core using an apple corer. Place a griddle pan or nonstick frying pan over a medium heat, add the pineapple in a single layer and cook for 3–4 minutes on each side until charred. Remove from the pan and repeat with remaining pineapple. Chop the pineapple into small chunks, place in a bowl and squeeze over the juice of 2 limes. Add 2 tablespoons chopped mint and mix well. Serve immediately.

3 Griddled Pineapple Kebabs with Chilli and Mint Syrup

Prepare the pineapple as above and cut into cubes. Thread on to 8 metal skewers and place in a shallow dish. To make the chilli syrup, place 1 medium red chilli, deseeded and thinly sliced, the grated rind and juice of 1 lime, 125 g (4 oz) golden caster sugar and 150 ml (¼ pint) cold water in a saucepan and stir over a low heat until the sugar has dissolved. Bring to the boil, then reduce the heat and simmer for 10 minutes until syrupy. Allow to cool slightly, then stir in 3 tablespoons chopped mint. Pour over the pineapple and leave to stand for 5 minutes. Preheat a griddle pan until hot, add the kebabs and cook for 8 minutes, turning occasionally. Serve 2 kebabs per person with any remaining syrup.

Instant Raspberry Sorbet

Serves 4

300 g (10 oz) frozen raspberries
2 tablespoons caster sugar
2 tablespoons water
1 tablespoon crème de framboise
  (raspberry liqueur) (optional)
fresh raspberries, to serve

- Place the raspberries, sugar, measurement water and crème de framboise, if using, in a food processor. Blitz for 2–3 minutes until all the ingredients are blended and start to come together.

- Serve scoops of sorbet immediately in bowls with fresh raspberries or place in a freezerproof container and freeze until ready to use.

 Raspberry Sorbet Meringues

Make the raspberry sorbet as above. Spread 1 tablespoon of the sorbet on each side of 2 meringue shells, then sandwich them together. Place in the freezer. Repeat with 6 more meringue shells. Remove from the freezer and serve immediately, drizzled with a little shop-bought fruit coulis.

Raspberry Sorbet Chocolate-dipped Cones Melt 50 g (2 oz) plain dark chocolate, broken into small pieces, in a heatproof bowl set over a saucepan of gently simmering water. Remove from the heat and dip the ends of 4 waffle cones into the melted chocolate, then roll the ends in 50 g (2 oz) chopped pistachios. Stand in glasses and chill until set. Make the raspberry sorbet as above and serve in scoops in the cones.

30 Tropical Fruit Salad with Ginger Green Tea Syrup

Serves 6

2 large mangoes, peeled, stoned and cut into 2.5 cm (1 inch) chunks

2 large papaya, peeled, seeds removed and cut into chunks

1 small pineapple, skinned, cored and cut into 2.5 cm (1 inch) chunks (see page 242)

2 kiwi fruit, peeled and cut into chunks

410 g (13 oz) can lychees, drained

250 g (8 oz) green grapes

For the syrup

125 g (4 oz) caster sugar

300 ml (½ pint) water

grated rind and juice of 1 lime

2.5 cm (1 inch) piece of fresh root ginger, peeled and chopped

1 green tea teabag

- To make the syrup, place the sugar, measurement water, lime rind and juice and ginger in a saucepan and heat gently, stirring occasionally, until the sugar has dissolved. Bring to the boil and simmer for 5 minutes.

- Remove from the heat and add the teabag, then leave to infuse for 10 minutes. Remove the teabag and pour into a jug. Chill for 10 minutes to allow the syrup to infuse and cool.

- Place all the prepared fruit in a large bowl and strain over the cooled syrup. Serve immediately or chill until ready to serve.

 Tropical Fruit Kebabs

Prepare 2 mangoes, 1 papaya and 1 pineapple as above and cut into cubes. Drain a 410 g (13 oz) can of lychees and thread with the prepared fruit, alternately, on to 12 metal skewers. Place on a baking sheet and sprinkle with the grated rind and juice of 2 limes and 2 tablespoons soft light brown sugar. Cook under a preheated hot grill for 3–4 minutes or until the sugar starts to caramelize.

 Tropical Fruits with Passion Fruit Syrup Place 6 tablespoons water and 2 tablespoons caster sugar in a small saucepan and stir over a low heat until the sugar has dissolved, then add 2.5 cm (1 inch) piece of peeled and sliced fresh root ginger. Simmer for 3 minutes, then leave to cool for 10 minutes. Meanwhile, prepare 2 mangoes, 2 papaya and 1 small pineapple as above and cut into thin rounds. Place the syrup in a blender and add the pulp and seeds of 4 passion fruit, then whizz for 10 seconds. Pour the syrup over the fruits and serve immediately.

 Gooseberry and Elderflower Fools

Serves 4

450 g (14½ oz) gooseberries
4 tablespoons elderflower cordial
50 g (2 oz) caster sugar
400 ml (14 fl oz) half-fat
  crème fraîche

- Place the gooseberries, cordial and sugar in a saucepan and bring to the boil, then partially cover with a lid. Simmer for about 8 minutes or until soft.

- Transfer to a food processor or blender and whizz until smooth. Pour into a large bowl and chill for 5 minutes until cool.

- Place the crème fraîche in a bowl and stir in two-thirds of the gooseberry purée. Spoon the fool into 4 glasses and top with the remaining purée. Serve immediately or chill until ready to serve.

 Gooseberry and Elderflower Compote Place 450 g (14½ oz) gooseberries, 4 tablespoons elderflower cordial and 3 tablespoons sugar in a saucepan and simmer, uncovered, for 8–10 minutes, stirring occasionally. Add a little more sugar to taste if necessary. Serve with dollops of fromage frais.

Gooseberry and Elderflower Crumble Place 700 g (1 lb 7 oz) gooseberries in a 1.2 litre (2 pint) ovenproof dish. Sprinkle over 75 g (3 oz) caster sugar and 2 tablespoons elderflower cordial. Place 100 g (3½ oz) wholemeal flour and 75 g (3 oz) low-fat spread in a bowl and rub together with the fingertips until the mixture resembles fine breadcrumbs. Alternatively, use a food processor. Stir in 100 g (3½ oz) muesli and 2 tablespoons caster sugar. Sprinkle the topping over the fruit and press down lightly. Place in a preheated oven, 180°C (350°F), Gas Mark 4, for 20–25 minutes until golden and bubbling.

Index

Page references in *italics* indicate photographs

Acknowledgements

Executive editor: **Eleanor Maxfield**
Senior editor: **Leanne Bryan**
Copy-editor: **Jo Murray**
Art director: **Jonathan Christie**
Design: **www.gradedesign.com**
Art direction: **Juliette Norsworthy & Tracy Killick**
Photographer: **Will Heap**
Home economist: **Denise Smart**
Stylist: **Isabel De Cordova**
Senior production controller: **Lucy Carter**